RREKGETSI CHIMELOANE

Who's laetie are you?
My Sowetan boyhood

KWELA BOOKS

Copyright © 2001 Rrekgetsi Chimeloane
c/o Kwela Books
28 Wale Street, Cape Town 8001;
P.O. Box 6525, Roggebaai 8012

All rights reserved
No part of this book may be reproduced or transmitted in any form or by any means, electronic, electrostatic, magnetic tape or mechanical, including photocopying, recording, or by any information storage and retrieval system, without written permission of the publisher

Cover design and typography by Louw Venter
Book design and typesetting by Nazli Jacobs
Set in 10.5 on 14pt Photina
Printed and bound by NBD
Drukkery Street, Goodwood, Western Cape
First edition, first printing 2001

ISBN 0 7957 0123 3

This book is dedicated to all those young souls who survived the township to become the adults of today. There is a belief in Soweto that if you were raised in the township and have never been robbed, beaten, sworn at or conned, then you haven't lived.

Contents

Hanky-panky	9
Territorial obstacles and dangerous dogs	19
"Seeing bioscope"	29
Sweets, snacks and lunch money	42
Lower Primary	48
Levi and I	59
Work and play	69
Thieves, thugs and rascals	82
Passing away	90
School outings	94
Hostilities and altercations	99
Eating around	107
1976: The "Power" and visiting Pylkop	112
Goodbye to boyhood	131
Word list	135

Hanky-Panky

"Wa phapha, wena!" I berate Mirabel. "You have a big mouth, wena Mirabela."

I was furious that afternoon. Word was out on the streets long before I had even zipped up my short khaki pants. By the time I emerged from Levi's outside toilet, followed by his sister Nokuthula, the word had spread like wildfire. The one who fanned the blaze was Mirabel. That overcast afternoon, during the April school holidays of 1971, all those who were around my neighbourhood in Diepkloof Zone Four, Soweto, near Sedibeng sa Thuto Lower Primary School, looked at me and shook their heads.

At the tender age of seven, I understood that what Nokuthula and I had done in their toilet was wrong. But I was bewildered at the response, especially from those bigger boys who were old enough to be my brothers. Their reaction was almost the opposite of what I had grown to expect regarding the pranks of silly boys like me. At that time children were accountable not only to their biological parents but to all parents at large, as well as to anyone old enough to be their older brothers or sisters. I thought the older boys would draw their belts and punish me for my deeds, but all they did was shake their heads and smile.

I had all sorts of stones ready in my hands with the intention of driving Mirabel away from our fence where she stood relaying the news to my sisters.

"I am telling you," she shouted at the top of her voice, one hand resting against her waist while the other was performing aerobics in the air as if to give added flair to her narration of what happened in the toilet. My sisters, Pontsho and Lesego, who were two and four years older than me respectively, were swiftly approaching the gate where Mirabel stood. The expressions on their faces were those of people hungry to swallow every juicy inch of the news.

"Move the hell away from our gate," I shouted at the top of my voice. How I wanted to crush her with my stones. The only thing stopping me was the fact that she was physically disabled. I looked at her inward twisting black orthopaedic left boot with its myriad belts and laces and the two-inch-thick sole that looked heavy enough to weigh down a house, and was quickly reminded how I had been taught to respect people with a physical disability. I had a brother, Gilbert, who was in that state. Looking at her now and feeling the stones in my hand, I knew I was not going to be able to fulfil my wishes.

"Alex and Nokuthula had a good round of hanky-panky in Levi's toilet," Mirabel reported when my sisters were standing right next to her, her voice still loud enough to be heard by all the neighbours.

But even more disturbing was the fact that she was laughing as she recounted the full train of events to my sisters. She was obviously not aware of the repercussions of her big mouth, I thought. If the story reached my mother's ears when she returned home from work, I was going to be in a lot of trouble. Knowing my mother as I did, she was not going to wait for an explanation; in a jiffy, she would be all over me with a peach tree stick. But that of course also rested on my sisters' willingness to tell my mother. I knew from past experience that they could also take another tack and decide not to tell my mother and blackmail me over the incident for the rest of my boyhood. Just like they did with a weakness I had of wetting the blankets. "We will tell your friends you wet the blankets – o rotela dikobo," was how they used to threaten me, in most cases to get me to do things around the house that I blankly refused to do, like washing dishes after lunch when my mother was not around. Now this incident of the toilet escapade was going to put them in a stronger bargaining position than ever before. Whichever way I turned, it seemed I was a loser.

How could I have been that stupid to fall yet again for one of Levi's suggestions? It was not that long ago when my mother had punished me for drinking – at Levi's instigation – the last of the condensed milk in the jar. And here I was again, standing the chance of another punishment because of Levi.

I recalled seeing Levi's head poking through the bottom opening of the toilet door while I was busy negotiating the procedure with his sister. To tell the truth, Levi seemed to be watching and enjoying what we were doing. I remembered how his white teeth shone through the bottom part of the toilet door, which stopped twenty-five centimetres short of the floor.

What happened in that toilet was not my fault. I wasn't the sort of boy who had the guts to confront a girl and tell her that we should go and do "silly things". Nokuthula and her friends were the ones who always kept making fun of me, saying that I was a fool because I did not want konfyt – jam. I never saw any konfyt in their possession, hence I ignored them. But on that day, when Nokuthula offered to give me konfyt after being labelled a coward by her friends, I followed her, of course with Levi's enthusiastic nod of approval, to the lavatory. And then she said, "You show me yours and I will show you mine."

Although nothing happened, other than a surprised gawking, I knew that if my mother found out there was going to be hell to pay. Being a no-nonsense kind of person, there was no amount of explaining that was going to rescue me. I would be in serious trouble. My father rarely intervened in domestic matters. It was my mother's wrath I feared.

Unable to scare Mirabel off, I squatted on the pavement outside my house, which was on the corner opposite Sedibeng sa Thuto Lower Primary School's main gate, my pale legs protruding from my khaki shorts and my pale arms sticking out of my powder blue short-sleeved shirt with its missing buttons. As usual I was scruffy and dirty, the state of my dirtiness this time around the result of playing all morning at the dumping ground opposite the school's yard. Sitting there, I knew I had to come up with a plan, and fast. As my eyes fixed on the passage between the school's fence and Bra Tito's house, where my mother always appeared from on her way back from work, I tossed a few ideas around in my head.

Then it came to me. I rushed into our yard and headed straight for our steel bathtub. I began to pour water into the tub from the only tap which served our house, an outside tap next to our only toilet, an outside toilet, which stood about five metres away from our little square four-roomed home. I was going to do something I did not often do, I was going to surprise my mother by scrubbing myself clean before she had even arrived home. It was a good plan which I knew would win her favour. Unfortunately for me, though, the bath was leaking, from a hairline crack at the seam between the base and the body. It was the same steel bathtub I had taken only a week before to Ntate – Mr – Moja for soldering.

I recall how I waited there, watching him with his unkempt hair and bushy beard, dressed in his dark brown boiler suit and pale reef boots as he fired up his paraffin soldering torch and started his work. Every time the soldering was finished he would send me to fetch a jug of water to pour into the bath to see if the leak was fixed. This procedure was carried out several times before the job was finally successful.

"Take Mma – Mother – Zondi's bath as well," Ntate Moja pointed to a small bathtub on top of a heap of other steel containers which included kettles, pots, and other bathtubs of all kinds and sizes. "You must tell her that it was only a small problem, and ..." he stopped and took out a pipe from the front chest pocket of his boiler suit and with his big rough hands he filled it gently with a black bush that resembled his beard and which he drew out from the same pocket, "... and tell her it is all fixed up now. She can send my payment through."

"Remain in peace, Ntate Moja." I said goodbye with two tubs in my little hands and left.

Now there I was in my back yard, desperately trying to get clean before my mother came home, stuck with a tub that was supposed to have been repaired days ago. With an idea in my head to temporarily fix the problem, I went into the house and was stopped dead in my tracks by my sister, Lesego.

"You just throw yourself in here without wiping your dirty feet first," she yelled at me. Lesego had a sharp tongue and had a way of always snapping at me.

I looked down at the shining multi-coloured vinyl kitchen tiles at my feet and did not see the marks I was supposed to have made. I stubbornly took a step inside.

"What is this one doing?" My sister Pontsho now stood behind Lesego, both her hands tucked into her waist.

"I do not see dirt on ..."

"Even if you do not, go back and wipe your feet." Lesego was wagging a finger at me. "I am going to tell Mma what you did with Nokuthula today."

I stepped back reluctantly, reversing to the doormat at the back door, and started wiping my feet thoroughly. As my one foot was airborne, Pontsho stopped me again.

"Wait just there," she rummaged around behind the coal stove and returned with a skroplap – old cloth for washing floors. "There!" she threw it at me. "Wipe those tracks from the floor."

"But I do not see ..."

"Hei wena!" Lesego screamed at me. "Come here." She beckoned me with a forefinger that was flicking back and forth as she stood in the doorway leading into our dining cum sitting room. Then she started pointing downwards.

I looked at her for a moment and then at Pontsho, anger building inside me as I watched both of them savouring every inch of what they were up to. It was a rare opportunity for them and they had to make the most of the situation. They knew, as well as I, that under normal circumstances, they wouldn't mess with me like this. But now they had a hold on me, and it appeared as if they were sinking their fangs into me for all the cheek and mischief I had given them in the past. I eventually followed the direction of Lesego's downward-pointing finger.

"Look at that," she said, continuing to point her finger until I could finally make out my dirty tracks on the shining tiles.

Like an obedient altar boy, I went down on my knees and started wiping off the muddy prints. As I was about to rise to my feet, Pontsho stopped me again. Without saying anything, she pointed to a footmark I had missed. I lowered my head, looked at the muddy print and then at my two sisters. I threw the skroplap on the mark and began to wipe it with my one foot pressing down on the thick old cloth.

I knew that wiping with one's feet was never regarded as truly wiping. I enjoyed looking at my sisters' faces as they so obviously tried to figure a way to force me to stop using my foot. I recalled the day one of my mother's friends stopped me from doing just that. Personally, I preferred using my foot as opposed to kneeling, and could not see why it did not do just as good a job. "That is not the way to clean the floor, my boy," the woman said. "You have to use your hands." Angrily I glared at her, and felt like asking her, "Who the hell do you think you are to come and give me orders in my home?" But I could not do that, not with my mother standing nearby. Instead I obeyed her and did the right thing, knowing that if I did otherwise, my mother would dish out instant punishment. Insubordination towards elderly people, no matter what the reason, was just not tolerated as far as my mother was concerned.

Nonetheless, in front of my sisters now, I spitefully continued wiping the floor with my foot, just to rub them up the wrong way. When I had finished, I patted and moulded the skroplap into a ball and held it in my right hand. My facial expression changed into a nasty one and I saw the sudden panic on my sisters' faces. Knowing me as they did, they were aware of how easily I could have them scattering around the kitchen by using the ball of skroplap as a missile. I eyed them meanly as I bounced the skroplap from one hand to the other. All of a sudden they were no longer in control and their threats were not going to protect them from what I might do to them at any moment. My eyes moved from one to the other and then, as if to show them how lucky they were and that I was letting them off the hook, I unleashed the ball of skroplap but threw it against the front wall, where it landed behind the back of the stove. As my sisters turned and ran I disappeared into the dining room and returned with a fresh bar of Sunlight soap. I walked outside and temporarily patched the leak in the tub by rubbing layers of slightly dampened soap against the area where it was cracked.

I filled the tub and then made sure I scrubbed myself until there was some complexion on my dark face. If there was one day I did not want to draw my mother's attention to anything that was offensive about me, this was the day. After my bath I washed out the tub thoroughly and even changed my clothes, which I normally refused to change on a regular basis. You should have seen how clean I looked that day, my tiny black face shining with Vaseline petroleum jelly, which I rubbed on straight after my bath. Then I sat on the front stoep and waited nervously for my mother. I kept my eyes on the passage next to Bra Tito's house, where she would appear. It was not long before I saw her approaching with a heap on her head and parcels in both her hands. I ran like a bat out of hell to meet her.

"Dumela, Mma," I greeted politely and immediately relieved her of a couple of parcels from her hands.

"Dumela, Alex, what did you do today?"

I nearly froze. I was not sure if she had already heard the news about the shenanigans of the day.

"I ... I did nothing today, Mma," I responded hesitantly.

"You look nice," she said without turning, as she had to balance the load that was on top of her head.

"I have washed already, and ... and I have also changed my clothes." Anticipating the disturbing news that could come her way at any moment, I wanted to make sure she was aware of my good deeds of the day. Out of the corner of my eye, I caught her smile, and I felt relieved.

After she had unloaded her baggage on the kitchen table, I asked, "Don't you want me to go and buy fresh milk for you, so that I can make you some tea, Mma?"

"Hau!" Lesego exclaimed. "Why are you being so nice today, when normally we have to hunt for you to go to the shops?"

"Sometimes we literally have to drag you so that you will go to the shops," put in Pontsho.

Normally I would have reacted, perhaps even taken out the skroplap again, but that day I just kept quiet. I did not even unleash a single word from my vulgar tongue. I had one intention and one intention only, to avoid creating any scene whatsoever that might bring forth the sordid details of my affair with Nokuthula.

On my return from the shops, I watched every move around the house in case my sisters had related the story to my mother in my absence. I did not want to be caught off guard or walk into a trap, something which my sisters were quite capable of planning, because they knew that in a one-on-one pursuit, if it came to that, neither of them could catch me.

That day I became a sweet boy. I made my mother tea just as she liked it. She liked it to brew for a while before it was served, which meant I first had to pour in the tea leaves and then only could I add the boiling water – something which normally made not an iota of difference to me. In addition to that, I had to keep the metal kettle away from the hottest part of the coal stove, to prevent it from boiling, and I had to boil the milk four times. Every time the milk boiled I had to remove it for a minute and then place it back on the stove again. My mother said this procedure prevented the left-over milk from going off as we did not even have the luxury of a paraffin fridge, which, considering most of us never had electricity, was in itself an item for the well-to-do in Soweto at that time. She also wanted lebebe, the thick layer that formed on top of the milk after it had been boiled. My mother used to say, "Gape nna ke nyetswe ka dikgomo," meaning that her lobola – bride's wealth – was not paid in cash but in cattle, hence she had the sole right in our house to eat lebebe. If I was not trying to be nice that day, I could easily have picked up that thick layer of cream with a spoon and thrown it in my mouth, as I often did. Afterwards I would always claim that, on that particular occasion, the milk did not produce such a layer. But today was different; I did not want to rattle the boat.

"Can I have another cup?" my mother asked, sitting on the chair outside the house, next to the kitchen door. "Sometimes I forget how excellent your tea can be."

I just nodded, as I quickly swept the cup and saucer from her hands and vanished into the kitchen, soon to return from the hot stove with another cup.

"Mma, do you want me to cut your toenails?" I knew she liked that and sometimes asked me to cut them.

"I wonder why someone is being so nice today!" Lesego exclaimed, looking to Pontsho, who was standing beside her.

"Maybe it's something that someone did this afternoon?" Pontsho said.

I kept stoically quiet as if I did not hear the remarks, and I quickly returned to my mother's side with a nail clipper.

"Mma," Lesego called. "Did Alex tell you what happened today?"

Oh-oh, that didn't sound good at all, I thought, and knew I had to do something very quickly.

"These two have been ill-treating me all day, Mma," I started crying. "I do not know what they want from me ..."

"You two leave your little brother alone," my mother came to my defence. "Don't you know that this is my grandfather. He was named after my great-great-grandfather, my father's father's grandfather.

Stop pestering him if you do not want to make me angry. This is my last-born and I do not want to hear any more of this happening."

I was making faces at my sisters as my mother lifted me and placed me on her lap. She poured me tea in a saucer and blew on it to cool it down. She gave me the saucer like a real baby and I sipped at it carefully, smiling all the time. I knew my secret was safe, at least for that day.

Territorial obstacles and dangerous dogs

On some days students attended "morning classes" and on other days "afternoon classes". This did not bother me, as long as I remembered which week I should be at school at what time. The times were either in the morning, starting at eight o'clock, or still in the morning, starting at eleven o'clock. Don't ask me why eleven o'clock was referred to as afternoon ... I liked both morning and afternoon classes as they both presented advantages to me. In the case of morning classes, I could play at the playgrounds after school until the afternoon pupils were let out, and then go home with them.

Walking home alone after morning classes had its problems. Especially for someone like me who was at Ikaneng Lower Primary School, which was about four kilometres away from where I lived. Having to walk back home with the streets deserted, except for the school-dodgers, drop-outs and bullies, was never an easy task. To make matters worse, there were not only boundaries between each of the suburbs or "townships", as we called them, of Soweto, but there were also invisible boundaries between each of the zones which made up the different "townships". On top of that, in many cases there were invisible borders within the zones. Diepkloof had six zones, all of them, in one way or another, hostile to one another. In Diepkloof this meant that walking from Zone Four, which was where I lived, to

Zone Three had certain hazards. The Zone Three boys, if they spotted you, would chase you all over the place and then beat the hell out of you – that is, if you were too slow or your tactics of manoeuvre were not up to scratch.

I do not think any person who grew up in a township can tell you how one distinguished between residents of one zone and another, given the large number of people who resided in the area. You could simply *see* the difference.

One day I saw doves flying low above my house. I was with my friends and I took a stone and was about to throw it at the doves.

"Ijo, ijo, ijo. O tla go gata Joe, ka majuba a gage!" One of my friends, Jimmy, warned me that Joe would beat me into the dust if I hit one of his doves. How it was possible to distinguish between wild doves and local doves was beyond me, but it was, and distinguishing between people of different zones was a piece of cake by comparison.

One thing that I never understood, though, was the animosity we displayed towards things strange, especially animals. The mere sight of something strange translated into castigation of the highest order.

Ikaneng Primary School, which I attended from 1971 to 1974, and where along with my lessons, I learnt to wear a tie.

I recall how we used to stone strange dogs to death. There were even stone-throwing specialists when it came to stray animals. Dimros was one of them. He had a reputation of delivering a deathblow with a single half-brick thrown at a poor animal.

Coming back to boundaries, there were, as I said, even invisible borders within zones, and Zone Four, where I lived, was no different. It also had its territorial borders. There was "ko Modise o Botse", which was the area next to a church called Modise o Botse; there was "ko digroundeng", which was the area next to the Diepkloof soccer fields; there was "ko dishopong", which was the area next to the café; there was "ko di olopreineng", which was the area next to Baragwanath Airport; and lastly there was "ko maeneng", which was the area next to the mine dumps.

Ikaneng, where I went to school, was a stone's throw away from "next to Zone Three", whereas I lived in Zone Four, next to the "Baragwanath Airport" side. The most dangerous spots in any of the zones were "passages" that made one's journey shorter. Passages were dangerous for everyone, including us kids, but mostly they were dangerous at night. That was when murders and robberies took place in and around passages.

There was this one passage which I had to use on my way to and from school. There were no viable alternative routes. For example, with the main alternative route you had to go by the shops first and then follow Immink Drive for about a kilometre, until you turned into the street where the school was; this route was very long and even worse than the normal short-cut I took when it came to unruly elements. Tactically, the worst part about this alternative route was that you did not have many ways out if bullies or territory-mongers gave you chase, because it was mainly one long straight street.

Also, what made the passage on this particular route painfully memorable to me was a series of accidents I experienced on it. I was knocked down by a bicycle three times in that passage. And on all three occasions I sustained head injuries. I really cannot explain how the accidents occurred. All I knew was that if I was on that passage and a bicycle entered the passage at the same time, it was certain that no matter which side I ran to, I would end up with my head graced by the spokes of the bicycle's wheels.

In such cases, whenever I reached home, I would go straight to the tap and pour water all over my head and face to disguise as best I could my injuries. I did not want my two sisters seeing me in that "mess" for fear of being mocked. I also had to make sure that none of my four older brothers saw me, because I knew they would label me a sissy who could not stand up to his equals. So every time I came home after an "accident" or a fight, especially if I had lost, I would head straight for the tap to rub away the marks, tears, and the red-hot prints that remained on my cheeks from the short, sharp, flat-handed blows to the face that were known to us as "claps".

The other obstacle along all of the alternative routes was my biggest nemesis, dogs. They really made my life hell. I had to remember all the routes I used not only for the potential bullies in the area but also for the dogs resident on those routes.

Yes, I was terrified of dogs.

I have no idea what I did to warrant such hostility from members of the canine species. The simple reality was that from as far back as I could remember, dogs did not like me. They seemed repulsed by my appearance. My friends and I could be walking down the street, less than a foot apart, but if there was a dog about, I would be the one who was attacked.

There was one dog in particular, five houses away from my house, a black and white little thing called Spotty, which made my life a nightmare. One of my mother's distant cousins, Mma Kumako, lived next door to the house where Spotty lived. Every time my mother sent me with a message to her, there was no other way but to pass by that dog's home. To make matters worse, where that dog lived was also at the beginning of my route to school and my route to the shops. This meant that I had to come into contact with Spotty almost every day.

Everybody always told me, "That is a harmless dog and it will never bite you. Just don't run away when you see it." The problem with those people was that they did not see the dog through my eyes. If they had watched the movie, The Doberman Gang, they would be keeping their ideas to themselves. I mean, how could I be expected just to stand there facing a set of shining, sharp white teeth, an unforgiving growl, and the wild glint in the eyes of that black and white dog?

Good as I was with stones, I could not stone Spotty. Stoning it would translate into a variety of undesirable repercussions, for example, the owners coming to tell my folks that I was abusing their dog, or Skumbuzo, their young son, retaliating by beating me up. Not that I was afraid of Skumbuzo by himself, but Skumbuzo and his cousin Muzi were inseparable, and if you added the dog to this duo, you ended up with a formidable opponent. My somewhat fragile, asthmatic body was a poor match.

One day, as usual, my mother sent me to her distant cousin, Mma Kumako's, to ask her where their next women's sosaete – social club – would be. At that time there were almost no phones in black residential areas. I had only ever seen a phone in the movies. So a simple question could cost one up to an hour's walk or more – and usually it was the duty of the youngest, like me, to deliver the messages. Given the intricacies of territorial borders, and other considerations such as dogs, I did not like being sent to convey messages.

My mother did not want to know about these dilemmas. All she was interested in was for the message to be delivered and getting the feedback as soon as possible. If I ever complained that I was going to be beaten by other boys, her reply would be, "Why don't you hit them back?" She did not know that it was not as simple as that. For one thing, you did not hit back in foreign territory; you humbled yourself even to the idiots and weaklings, with the hope that one day, if by some luck fate should deliver them into your domain, you would catch them and dish out revenge.

Another woman my mother used to send me to with messages,

was Mma Mojapelo, who lived in Diepkloof Zone Three. Zone Three also had its subsections. She lived in the area called Ghost Town. This Ghost Town was not the kind of ghost town that had been deserted by its inhabitants. This one was different, because it was overcrowded with inhabitants. On top of which, Ghost Town was right next to an area called Jerusalem ... yes, Jerusalem. Young people called the area Mjerujeru. If you never thought there could be anything holy around Soweto, especially in Diepkloof for that matter, think again. There it was, a mine dump called Jerusalem. How a mine dump in Diepkloof's backyard came to be blessed with the name of the Holy City, I have no idea. But there were those who claimed that there were freebies, meaning free sweets, at Mjerujeru. Us boys simply believed it when the older boys told us that they got a lot of sweets at the mine dump. Some boys even claimed they had stumbled onto a utopia of freebies and the best of all these freebies were the "chunks of sweets". It was not difficult to believe them after seeing Pitso and his friend returning from Mjerujeru with handloads of sweets and ending up selling them to us.

Mjerujeru (Jerusalem), where the monumental setabola-nnyoko sweets mysteriously originated.

Among the different sweets they had for sale was this one monumental sweet called setabola-nnyoko, meaning "the one that tears the gall apart". The sweet, which boys like us loved to suck, was one big chunk of red crystal that was jagged at the edges but tasted sweeter and smoother than sugar. The adventurers to Mjerujeru had the sweet up for sale at five cents a chunk, which was way above what we could afford. All I could dream of was accompanying them on their next expedition so I could lay my hands on some free setabola-nnyoko. Of course I would have to do it without the knowledge of my mother. She always warned me not to eat too many sweets as my stomach reacted rather negatively to lots of sugar.

If my mother ever found out that I had been eating setabola-nnyoko she would not hesitate to give me castor oil. Castor oil was a thick, and I mean thick, oily laxative with an aftertaste that left me nauseous for a week. If there was one thing I hated among all the medications I had to take at that age, it was castor oil. My mother used to tell me it was good for cleaning my stomach, which was made dirty by all the sweets I liked to eat. On the other hand, though, it has to be said that castor oil was better than spyt – the syringe. Spyt was used for the same purpose as castor oil, only with spyt one did not have to wait before visiting the toilet. In fact it was administered as close to the toilet as possible, because after the mixture – of water and Sunlight soap – was injected up one's backside, everything would come gushing out at almost exactly the same time. With castor oil, one would have to stay in bed and drink black tea and eat soft porridge in order to help the castor oil do its work. Also with castor oil, my mother would not allow me to flush the toilet until she had made sure the castor oil had done its job. This was because I used to secretly race to the toilet to vomit it out. My mother had cottoned on to this practice, hence the inspection. If she found the castor oil had not done its work, the exercise would have to be repeated the next weekend. My mother always said, "Gall will kill you, as it did Mma Mosweu's little boy."

Anyway, to get back to Ghost Town. It was right at the top end of

Diepkloof, next to Noordgesigt, and there was talk about paranormal activity in the area, including headless bodies that roamed the streets in the dark, and cars that sped along without drivers and caused havoc on the roads at night. What happened to Ghost Town at night was no concern of mine; what bothered me was the distance between my home and that of Mma Mojapelo, to whom I had to deliver my mother's messages. The distance was roughly six kilometres, which, as you can imagine, meant criss-crossing several foreign territories. Of course, at the time, public transport in the township was scarce. But even if taxis and buses were available, one of the main functions of children, especially young boys, was to be sent on errands. My mother used to say, "You think you will stay at home and the only thing you do will be eating? Come on ... your work is to be sent anywhere we want you to go. Or do you want me to go there by myself?"

This was what I hated most about being the last-born. My four brothers and two sisters, as well as my father and mother, could send me anywhere at will.

Before journeys like the one to Mma Mojapelo I would first canvass for backup from among my friends. There was one friend among the dozens I had who was always there for me, and that was Levi. He and I went through an assortment of street fights and mostly came out right side up. I had enemies all over, across zones and within zones, but they were few compared with Levi's. I do not know if he was attracted to adversaries or whether he just enjoyed making enemies. But he must have had five enemies for every one I had. Acquiring enemies was the simplest thing in those years, especially when there was little in the way of police or other forms of protection. You could quite innocently look at someone and be accused of looking at that person in the wrong way. The next thing you knew you were being chased. If you managed to outmanoeuvre your attacker, he would hunt you from that day on until he had satisfied himself that he had punished you in one way or another. So Levi and I would always line our pockets with stones and ketis – pocket-sized catapults – as weapons and ammunition for the potential fights we might encounter along the way. One's enemies had a way of popping up in very strange places. Sometimes they even resided at your very destination. Can you imagine thinking that you had outsmarted all your rivals on a six-kilometre walk, only to find one of them sitting in the kitchen where you were sent, drinking black tea with slices of brown bread? Well, it happened. In such cases, you had to deliver your message as quickly as possible, standing in the doorway, and then run for your life.

But, anyway, back to the day I was sent to my mother's distant cousin, Mma Kumako, which was just a few houses away. I approached the yard carefully looking out for Skumbuzo's dog, Spotty. Luckily it was nowhere to be seen and I was relieved. I delivered my mother's message and then rushed out of the house. As I hurried out of the yard, happy that I had survived the dog this time, there it was charging straight towards me. You should have seen how I accelerated. "Do not run away," someone shouted. "Just stay where you are," another voice called out. I thought, to hell with your advice and ran like a bat out of hell. The next thing I felt was something stinging my backside. As I looked back, there it was, Spotty, with its teeth sunk into my buttocks. I screamed like a baby as people started shouting at the dog, "Voetsek! Voetsek!"

Finally, scared off, the animal let go of me and strolled back into its yard, leaving me crying like a two-year-old until Kgorogo, Mma Kumako's young son, came and comforted me and led me back into their yard, where Mma Kumako administered her first-aid.

"Get the hair from the dog," Mma Kumako shouted to her son, pointing to the little black and white dog next door which had nearly torn me apart. When he had returned, she said to me, "Spit your saliva into my hand." I obeyed. Then she said, "Look that way," and pulled my short pants down and applied the mixture of saliva and dog's hair to my sore bottom.

I was escorted home that day by Kgorogo. My brothers laughed at me when they heard that I was chased and bitten by a little dog.

Why did it have to bite me in particular? A lot of people said that I was a nice boy. Even my sisters often told me that they wished I was a girl because I was so cute. My mother's friends also said that they wished they had small boys like me because I looked so loveable. But no, not to Spotty. You would think a dog with a name like that would be a cute little fluffy thing that you could cuddle. Not this one. All Spotty wanted to do was sink its teeth into my behind. That was its opinion of me being cute. As I sat there on that day, thinking about what had happened, I grew more and more angry with myself as I thought about how I allowed such a little dog to scare me. At the same moment something hit me – Sophia. She stayed opposite Mma Kumako's house. She was the girl of my dreams. She was soft-skinned and light in complexion and was the embodiment of beauty to me. I wondered whether she had witnessed the whole debacle. How would I approach her and tell her I wanted her to be my girlfriend, that is, if ever I gathered enough courage to do that? But if she saw me and that dog, she would probably laugh at me too, just like the rest of them. Worse still, she would probably laugh at me together with her friends in class. I could just imagine her telling her friends: "That stupid Alex was bitten by a little dog mo maragong" – on the buttocks.

I must get even with that dog, I told myself. Next time I walked near that house I would be carrying a half-brick concealed behind my back. One wrong move and I would strike it as hard as I could.

Since that day, Spotty, never bothered me again. Could it be that if it had just wanted to taste my backside?

"Seeing bioscope"

Thabang's uncle was Bra Hohle. Bra Hohle was the man who showed movies at Sedibeng sa Thuto, the lower primary school opposite our house. Soon all my friends started going to the movies, except me. How I wished I was related to Thabang who had free access to the movies on account of being Bra Hohle's nephew. As a non-relative, I would have to pay.

I asked my mother for twenty cents to go and "see bioscope", as we called it, and her reply was, "Bioscope shows you bad things. It will corrupt your mind."

"Have you seen Bruce Lee?" Levi would brag. He, Thabang, Jimmy and some of the other boys who were always going to see bioscope would go on and on about Bruce Lee and his kung fu.

"Why do you want to go to the movies?" my brother, Moropa, wanted to know when I asked him for the twenty cents I needed to go to the movies.

"Because all my friends go to the movies," I replied. What kind of answer did he expect from a nine-year-old?

"So," he said, as he busily chipped away at the golf balls on the front lawn, which he had nursed to the very un-Diepkloof-looking condition of a mini green, "if your friends were not going, you would also abstain?"

"Yes!" I quickly replied.

After all ten balls he had been chipping and putting away at were around the hole he had specially dug and manicured, I watched him swinging his club around his hand and remembered the day he and I took a photo on that same lawn. I was supposed to pose as his caddy with his black golf bag on my back. "Look at you," he snapped at me as I was trying to balance my little body under the weight of the enormous bag. "What kind of a caddy are you, who can't even hold the bag still?" Moropa ended up choreographing the whole photo-shoot that day.

Now I was experiencing the same feeling of being pushed around as I had during the day of the photo-shoot. "I think bioscope is not good for you," he said. "Most of the boys who go to bioscope either smoke dagga or sniff glue or benzene and get into all sorts of trouble. I suggest you let your friends go to the movies and you sit at home and read your school books."

What was I supposed to read in Standard One? "Benny and Betty" or "Matlhasedi" or … He should have just told me that he did not want me to go to the movies, finished and klaar. My oldest brother, Abuti – elder brother – Motsietsi, and my father were too far apart from me in age and ideas to even think of trying to ask them for money for the movies. As far as Abuti Motsietsi went, the only time I ever spent with him was when he was with his friend Mashego. They would play Elvis Presley or Percy Sledge songs on a battery-operated record player. I would watch in amazement and awe the pained and sombre look on their faces as they danced slowly across the room to the songs. I could not understand what it was in those songs that made them so sad.

At least my two middle brothers, Moropa and Kgofa, sometimes let me play cards with them, and I knew they were earning enough money from golf caddying to have some left over. As a result I took my chances with them. Unfortunately, as already seen, Moropa saw no benefits in my going to the movies, so that left me with only one last chance, Kgofa.

"I'll give you the money on one condition," Kgofa said as I looked at him with pleading eyes while he sorted through a handful of coins, "you wash my white Romika tekkies – sand shoes. Every time you have them clean and ready for me for the weekend, I will give you twenty cents."

The amazing thing was I had washed his tekkies many times before for free. So it was a bargain I just could not let pass. This was the beginning of a long contract with my brother Kgofa, that launched me into the fabulous world of movies. As time went on my appetite for movies only grew bigger and stronger, and unlike Moropa had predicted, I never smoked dagga, or sniffed glue or benzene.

The day I saw my first Bruce Lee movie – Enter The Dragon – I understood why all the boys were running around with two bits of stick loosely bound together at one end by a chain. Kung fu hit the township in a big way and almost all the boys around my age were shrieking and screeching out like Bruce Lee; now me included.

Most of my friends were a fair bit younger than me. I am not sure why, but I think it was the gentleness with which I interacted with the younger boys that made me a favourite among them. "He plays nice with us," Jimmy, one of my younger friends, once said to his mother. "He is not like the other bigger boys who always want to beat and make fun of us."

Of course the mismatch came at a price. As I was the oldest and tallest among my friends, I was always accused of leading them into mischief. As if that accusation were not enough, I also suffered immensely at the hands of other boys as I was automatically taken as the leader among my friends. Especially in battles with older kids, I was the one who was always picked on or beaten up. On the other hand, I also had to be the negotiator in those instances, and there were many of them, when my young friends messed up. Sometimes, when the going got tough and we had to run for our lives, I had to hold onto the hands of the most vulnerable and run with them, even if it compromised my own safety.

But, back to kung fu. I especially admired the boys who were going for karate and kung fu lessons all over the township. Every time I asked where I could go and sign up for classes, the other boys would look at me and say, "You think karate is for sissies like you? You wouldn't even last a minute there." There were boys who walked all the way to the Moravian Hall in Zone Five, about half an hour's walk through different zones and territories, for lessons, and I wished I was among them. Then I would never again be afraid of any threats or obstacles.

But in the end I stayed with the movies and admired the art of acting. The two genres that had the most impact on me, not surprisingly, were martial arts and cowboys and Indians movies. With the martial arts movies, not forgetting the special effects of actors performing the impossible, of great significance to me was the idea of seeing someone fighting bare-handed and defeating a bunch of people armed with a multitude of weapons. To me this was the answer to all the bullies who constantly threatened to beat me up with one weapon or another. The Hong Kong cinema presented me, in my mind anyway, with the possibility of turning myself from victim into victor. It showed me that you did not have to be big and strong to defeat your enemies, you just had to be quick and smart. Movies like Lady Whirlwind, with Angela Mao kicking all the bad guys from one end of the screen to the other, showed me that it did not even matter whether you were a boy or a girl.

One Arm vs. Nine Killers was another movie where someone who was meant to be weaker came out on top. In this movie the leading actor's hand was chopped off in a street battle and yet he still went on to defeat his opponents. These movies gave me courage in the face of pessimism and the fear of bullies, a fear that was not helped by the fact of my bad chest, a kind of asthma that I suffered from, which left me somewhat wanting in the realms of physical strength and endeavour. Not that I fared too badly. Only that I could have fared much better.

Naturally enough, as young boys we all started adopting role models from the big screen. However, when one talks of the big screen, people should not think that we had a conventional cinema. It was a township school hall – a makeshift movie house that existed on weekends only. What Bra Hohle did was to cover the windows with black plastic and throw a white sheet over the blackboard. That was our movie house, and since we had no other in the vicinity, that was fine with us.

Our first and foremost role model was Bruce Lee. As little boys we went crazy over Bruce Lee. What was strange, though, was that we could never remember even one of the names of the characters he played. To us, he was always simply known as Bruce Lee. Most of the other leading actors in the martial arts movies we gave names as we saw fit. We were around Sub B and Standard One and unable to remember or even properly pronounce their names, so we gave them names that seemed to suit their particular styles.

Take John Liu, for instance – due to his powerful kicking style, we called him Mr Ma-Kick. For some reason he was the only one ever afforded the respect of being called "Mr". I knew for a fact, because of the relatives we had living in the area, that in the Mabopane/Garankuwa district, north of Pretoria, he was called Chappies, after the bubble gum. Don't ask me why. But to the kids in those areas the name somehow must have made sense.

Those we never gave names were identified by their association with other actors and characters from the movies. It went something like, "He is the guy who was a friend of the starring who starred in the movie Eighteen Bronze Men." By "starring" we meant the leading actor.

You had to be clued up on martial arts movies the way we were to identify all the different characters. And don't believe people who tell you they cannot tell the difference between Chinese people because "they all look the same" – that is pure nonsense. Young as we were, with our narrow, generalising vision, we managed to identify all the different characters in the martial arts movies.

Another thing: we could not read the English subtitles at that age and were, anyway, not fast enough to follow the dialogue, but afterwards we could tell you exactly what the movie was about and what each character had said to the other.

What amazed me most, still amazes me as I look back, was how a movie that you had missed was related back to you with intricacy, flair and style by those who had seen it. You would be told exactly who said what to whom and would get a full demonstration of the action. A second-hand film narration went something like this:

"After the starring fought with the other man ... the one who was the villain in that other bioscope I told you about ..."

"Which bioscope was that?"

"That one I told you about last time, man ... about that man whose dark green punch sounded like a gun from the cowboy bioscope."

"Is it the same one who rode on a reed on top of the water and always said 'Buddha bless you' in the other movie we saw, when they showed us a double feature and the film burnt halfway, and we had to come back the next day and watched that other movie about Shaolin?"

"Yes, but this time he did not have that green fist. In this bioscope he could crush your skull with his bare hands ... "

"Yes, I remember that one ... "

You really had to know your stuff about martial arts movies to follow a narration like that, or perhaps you just had to be as young, naïve and easily excited as we were about action movies and the big screen.

A movie title we remembered by association with the "starring" or leading character in the movie.

"The starring is that old man ... uh, 'Gun Smoke' is his name," Levi, my best friend, informed me.

"Are you sure that's his name?" I inquired.

"Ma vra wao wao!" he swore, as we all did, on our mothers' reproductive organs. "His name is 'Gun smoke', you can ask anyone who saw the bioscope, they'll tell you."

One movie that still comes back to me is a martial arts version of the Marco Polo story. The movie had four reels instead of the standard three, which told us it was going to be longer than normal, and therefore you were getting more than your money's worth. During the first reel all I seemed to see was people in transit, travelling over wide stretches of barren land from one place to another, and not a single martial arts display. But there was another thing that stood out in that first reel; there seemed to be a white man moving around among all of these Chinese people. I figured he must be Marco Polo, as from my observations Marco Polo had to be white. His name was not only pronounceable, it was also English sounding. The more usual names we could never pronounce or recall … Cheng Xhing, Hseu Li, Fang Si Yu …

"No, he is not Marco Polo," Levi corrected me, having already seen the movie the day before. "You will see Marco Polo on the next reel."

For the whole first reel, no one was interested in the movie. There was no martial arts, which was what everyone had come to see, and secondly, most of the audience had already seen the movie the day before. But they had returned because they had made the movie the talk of the township. During the next reel, the whole room fell quite, as if instructed to do so by some higher force. And when one of the leading actors appeared, a fairly built oriental man, everyone suddenly started to whistle and cheer, and Levi said to me, "There, that is Marco Polo." Who was I to argue that he was not Marco Polo? And especially not at that moment, because from that moment on the film was full of the high-powered martial arts acrobatics that everyone had come to see, many for the second time.

Nevertheless, I was soon to learn that Levi was still wrong. The character Levi had said was Marco Polo was in fact a Shaolin fighting monk who went by a name that sounded something like "Chi Tu". I gathered this from Thabang who was sitting on the other side of me, banging my knee, saying, "Now you will see some action. You see him, ke ntja ntwana eo, shuu!" Thabang praised the Shaolin fighting monk, explaining to me that he was a die-hard kind of good guy – "a dog" – dog in the good sense of the word.

This mistaking of characters, actors and film titles stretched to all sorts of movies including American and British movies. We used to go to the shops on Friday afternoons to wait for Bra Hohle to come along and hang up the movie placards for the weekend. Because we could not yet read, we had to ask him what the name of the movie was, or if we missed Bra Hohle, we had to wait for one of the older boys to come. And we small boys listened to the bigger boys read from the movie placards, and took their word for whatever they came up with.

"*Shuu, shuu, shuu* ... Valdez Is Coming!" one of the older boys exclaimed with excitement after looking at the placards one Friday afternoon. "Butler 'n Castor ke ntja ka gun, moo." He told us how good "Butler 'n Castor" was with a gun in that movie.

To us, from then on, the famous actor Burt Lancaster was Butler 'n Castor. We ran along to those who had not yet seen the placards and told them how the movie that weekend had Butler 'n Castor in it, and how good he was with a gun, and they in turn ran on to others and spread the word about Butler 'n Castor.

With cowboy and Indian movies, we usually took the side of the bad guys, who were obviously the Indians. I do not know what prompted this spirit. It is easy now to think of it as sympathising with them on the basis of their fight against the white man, but I think the real reason had more to do with their courage in facing guns with tomahawks, hunting knives, and bows and arrows. Their prowess on horseback was another thing we could only dream of.

It was a sad day for us when we heard rumours that Bruce Lee had died.

"They said he used electricity for gym'ing" – working out – Thabang explained.

"You are lying," Levi argued. "How can someone use electricity for gym'ing?"

I was also puzzled by how anyone could use electricity for working out.

But Thabang, who was Bra Hohle's nephew, came close to proving his case by quoting from his famous movie-showing uncle. "I'm telling you, Levi. Malome – Uncle – Hohle told me that he was killed by electricity."

"I also heard that electricity can kill you if you pour water on it," I put my bit in. "My folks told me that electricity comes from water, that is why it is dangerous if you mix it with water."

"My father told me that you cannot see electricity," Levi defended. "Now how can Bruce Lee gym with it if you can't even see it?" On that knowing note Levi ended the argument.

After Bruce's death in 1973 the martial arts movie industry boomed. Hundreds of look-alike Bruce Lees began to appear everywhere. They even used similar names, like Bruce Le, and Bruce Li. But none of them quite caught our eye the way the true Bruce Lee did.

There also appeared a Gam Kwan Lee. Some of the bigger boys told us that his western name was Tommy Lee and that he was Bruce Lee's brother. We were so desperate for a successor to Bruce Lee that we believed them. But the only film in which we saw Tommy Lee was a movie called Bloody Ring. During the first reel the projector suddenly wound to a halt and Bra Hohle made his usual eloquent announcement: "Mamelang, mochini o robehile" – Listen, the machine is broken. The projector had broken down, as it often did, something we accepted as the norm. We settled for free tickets for the next weekend's movies. But that was the last we saw of "Tommy" Lee.

It wasn't too long after the departure of Bruce Lee, in the mid-seventies, that Hong Kong gave birth to another big screen sensation, Jackie Chan. The first time we saw Jackie Chan was enough to immortalise him in the minds of the young boys across Zone Four. The movie was Shaolin Wooden Men. We were mesmerised by the acrobatic spectacles and more especially by what we called his "snake style". Emerging from Shaolin Wooden Men, all of us were twisting ourselves trying to imitate him.

"What was the starring's name?" Levi asked.

"Shaolin," I answered confidently, once again mistaking the title of the movie for the main actor. It was only the first time we had seen Chan, and why shouldn't I have mistaken his name for the title of the movie? We had seen movies like Ben Hur, and the leading actor was "Ben Hur" to us for ever after. The same went for Hercules, Tarzan, Spartacus, Ivanhoe, and Spiderman. So logic told me that the name of the main actor must be Shaolin.

Week after week we practised, trying to imitate Jackie Chan, but we were never really successful. There was, however, this one little boy called Themba. He managed to emulate Jackie Chan almost to the letter. The way he mastered every move and its stylish synchronisation was something to die for. He was so good we ended up paying him what little bits of spare change we could lay our hands on just so that he would perform for us.

"Themba knows Shaolin style," the word spread all over the place. "He can do Shaolin for you."

I fell in love with the big screen so much that virtually my whole life revolved around going to the movies. At school we spoke about movies, and when we played we imitated characters we had seen on the screen. We adopted names from the movies, and in our play-fighting we called one another by those names. Movies became not only our main source of entertainment but also a good part of our education. The only time I missed out on going to the movies was midnight shows. The aim of midnight shows was to keep the smaller boys like us from seeing adult movies. I could not imagine what an "adult movie" was. Didn't it have people and cars, music and dancing, and kissing and all of those things?

"You boys are mad, you can't go and see midnight movies. You are still young," Pitso, one of Bra Hohle's helpers dismissed us while we were trying to put forward our case for being allowed into a midnight show. But this did not apply to Levi. Pitso, who was a good deal older than Levi, had recently become the boyfriend of Nokuthula – Levi's sister. Yes, the same one I had committed hanky-panky with in the toilet. For the first time Levi was not at war with

Pitso; they were in fact suddenly great buddies. Pitso's relationship with Nokuthula did not only see Levi gaining access to the midnight movies, but he also gained free entry to the other movies, just like Thabang.

I remember how Levi felt elevated above us all because he had been to the midnight movies and seen a film known to us as Highway Queen.

"What was in it?" Levi was asked as we grouped around him to hear the mysteries of the midnight movies.

"*Shuu!*" he breathed out with his hand across his mouth. He looked around to check if there were any adults approaching, then he said: "You won't believe it when I tell you."

"Please tell us," we pleaded, and pestered him to the point where some of us were prepared to go down on our knees to hear what was in the movie.

Levi was a pretty shrewd and wily character and was known to go overboard when he told stories. For example, once he told us about this movie where one character actually removed his head and held it under his arm and went like, "*Aaghh!* Why you troublemaker. This is my tlhogo – head – take!" And he handed his head to his adversary. In this case, his exaggeration had given him away. We knew that there was no way a Hollywood actor was going to mix English and Sesotho ... "this is my tlhogo" ... but we did not have much choice but to believe Levi. We had not seen the film ourselves and, anyway, the point was that it was exciting, different, and it was the movies. Knowing Levi as I did, there was always some exaggeration mixed in with some truth.

Once, on his return from an air show at Baragwanath Airport, Levi had told me: "I saw a white boy shitting." I could not understand why that was exciting, until Levi said, "His droppings were gold."

I looked at Levi unable to believe my ears, and asked, "Did you say gold?"

And as Levi replied, "It was shining ... gold," I suddenly believed him. It made sense. It made things much clearer. Now I understood why whites were so rich; they actually shat gold – the mystery solved at last. I understood why they had so much money and lived in huge houses and why all our folks had to go and work for them. I wondered what it was they ate in order to shit gold. I thought it would be a fantastic idea if one could but lay one's hands on whatever it was these people ate.

This idea of whites shitting gold also lent renewed truth and meaning to the hundreds of accolades our folks heaped on white children, especially our mothers who worked for them. It always went something like, "White children would never do such a thing," or "You'll never be like white children ... they are taught good manners, not like you," or "White boys are neat, they do not play on rubbish heaps like you do," or "White children always read their books when they get home from school, you won't see them gallivanting all over the place like you do," or "If you scrub yourself well, you will end up good like white boys."

I actually took the last statement literally. You should have seen how I used to go to town with a piece of flat stone and scrub away at my tiny black body. Who wouldn't want to become a white boy one day ... have lots of toys to give to black children and lots of ou klere – old clothes – to dish out to black folks. Now there they were again ... shitting gold ... the zenith of their never ending powers and capabilities. I just could not understand how come I turned out to be black. It would have been so nice to be a white boy ...

But to get back to Levi and the Highway Queen. As he finally related the story to us, there was a certain bewilderment in his face that suggested he himself was still reeling from the shock of what he had seen. Our eyes almost popped out of their sockets.

"You saw all of it?" Jimmy asked.

"Yes, right there, on the big screen," Levi replied, stretching out his hands to demonstrate the magnitude of it all.

"You want to tell me you saw the white woman's thing on the big screen?"

I had to be sure.

"He says they saw all of it." Thabang had suddenly turned into Levi's ambassador. "I wish I was there."

I also wished I could have seen that movie. I was afraid of the dark and of being out late at night, but to go and see the white woman's thing on a big screen, I would have braved the darkest night. Thinking back, I wonder what the Minister of Bantu Affairs would have said had he known that young black boys were seeing the missies' things sprawled all over the big screen in some small classroom in downtown Diepkloof, just like that. I am sure Bra Hohle could well have spent time on "The Island" for that.

Sweets, snacks and lunch money

Bullies literally paraded the streets and exercised their will with impunity. But they appeared, in our eyes anyway, more aggressive towards school children than anyone else. They knew for sure that no matter what, we had to go to school, and that meant crossing their territories. These bullies had strategic points where they blommed – hung around – waiting for the pupils of Ikaneng Lower Primary School, my school. Their favourite spots were the passages on both corners of Tlotlego Higher Primary School and the passage where I was always hit by bicycles.

Five cents sounds like nothing today, but back in the early seventies it was more than enough for a Standard One pupil like myself, and a fortune to lose if it was robbed off you by some bully, something which we all experienced at one time or another.

Five cents was my daily allowance ... if it was available. In my home it was the standard daily allowance for the primary school children.

Of my parents' eight children, four were still at primary school: Gilbert and Lesego, who were at Tlotlego Higher Primary School, and Pontsho and I who were at Ikaneng Lower Primary School, just a stone's throw away from Tlotlego Higher Primary.

My oldest sister, Ausie – older sister – Maki, also the oldest child in the family, had left home while I was still in crèche. The last time

I remember her presence at home was the day of her wedding. It was an overcast day and to tell the truth just about the only other thing I remember about the day was the fact that my mother kept insisting that we, the little ones, go and stay at our neighbours. She said that she wanted to get us out of "busy people's" way. As for how my sister looked in her wedding dress, the only recollection I have is from what I later saw in the photographs. Instead of watching the wedding, I was mostly interested in guarding the front gate to keep out boys who might want to gatecrash the wedding. It was the first time there was a function of such magnitude at our home, and I was merely doing what I saw other boys do whenever they had functions at their homes.

My oldest brother, Abuti Motsietsi, was already working and the other two, Kgofa and Moropa, were at Madibane High School in Diepkloof Zone Three. For Kgofa and Moropa daily monetary provision was not a problem because they both worked as golf caddies over weekends and earned more than enough money for themselves. I knew that because whenever I had morning classes I would rush home and wait for them to come in to "change books" at lunchtime for their afternoon lessons. On their way home, my brothers would pass by the shops and buy fat cakes, French polony, atchaar, and other tasty foods. Because Madibane High School was so far away from our house, they were always in a hurry and would only eat half of the food and leave the rest for me. That part of my brothers' lunchtime actually made me love morning classes. Not that I was complaining, but I never knew why my brothers did not take all the books they needed for all their lessons in one shot. Later I learnt that it was the norm. High school kids preferred carrying the books they needed for specific lessons in the morning and afternoons separately. There were too many books for them to carry around in a school bag for the whole day and there were no school lockers for them to store books in. As a result, they did not use school bags like us little ones and always carried their books in their hands. To us little ones, a person carrying books in their hands represented the very pinnacle of learning. I looked forward to the day I would be carrying a few books under my armpit as well.

As to money and the four of us who were at primary school, there was never any certainty that we would receive our daily allowance. We had to depend on our parents for our five cents daily fare, and sometimes, for one reason or another, my father would not leave the four five-cent pieces for us before he trundled off to work. We never liked it when this happened, but we were well aware that we went to a school where there were many children who never received any money at all for food. For these children lunch-break was used for playing only, not eating.

Nevertheless, to ensure that we did not miss out, my sisters and I invented a verse for reminding our father about our daily allowance. Our father, like most at that time, was not the sort of person you just approached straight out and asked for money or things. Protocol was strictly adhered to and the chain of command had to be followed. Even if we were required to go on a school trip, I would have to ask my mother and she would then negotiate the necessary money for me with my father. If he agreed, he would hand me the money personally.

To remind our father about our daily allowance, my sisters and I would recite aloud, from the dining room where we slept, the verse we had specially made up. My parents slept in one bedroom, my four brothers crammed into the other bedroom, while my two sisters and I turned the dining room into a bedroom at night. Whenever we had visitors who slept over the three of us had to move into the kitchen and give over the dining room to the visitors.

The verse we recited went like this:
Alex: Re!
Pontsho: Ko!
Lesego: Pa!
Alex: Che!
Pontsho: Le!
Lesego: Te!

Alex: Ya!
Pontsho: Go!
Lesego: Ja!
Alex: Ko!
Pontsho: Se!
Lesego: Ko!
Alex: Lo!
Pontsho: Ng!

The words meant, "We are asking for lunch money for school." We would repeat the verse several times before we stopped.

Five cents was a lot of money. For instance, I could buy ye-belungu – "the white man's" – for two cents. The reason for the term I do not know, but ye-belungu was a peanut butter sandwich with a mug of milk, which was provided to schools by the African Children's Feeding Scheme. Perhaps the name was a play on the nature of the feeding scheme. Anyway, since "the white man's" cost only two cents, and I had five, I would spruce up my sandwich with a spoonful of atchaar that cost one cent and was sold by an old lady who sat a few metres away from where the ye-belungu kombi parked. To this day, peanut butter and atchaar sandwiches remain one of my favourite snacks.

When I went to afternoon classes there was no ye-belungu, as the van only came once in the morning, around ten o'clock. With the afternoon classes we used to buy fat cakes, atchaar and polony. Alternatively, there was an old man who lived two houses away from the school's main gate. He used to sell mosoko-buns. A mosoko-bun was something like a small Christmas cake. I enjoyed it very much. The only problem with mosoko-buns was their scarcity, as the old man could not always be relied on to make them, or did not have any left in stock when you wanted to buy them.

I was cautious about how I spent my remaining two cents once the ye-belungu and atchaar were paid for. Usually I kept it for buying sweets at the shops on my way back from school. With two cents you could buy so many sweets it was unbelievable. One of my favourites was a toffee called "butterflies". With one cent you could buy four of them. My other favourites were "chocolate toffees" and "banana rolls", which sold at two for one cent.

Sometimes I used my remaining two cents on a packet of fish crumbs or fish bread. Fish bread was a slice of bread fried in fish oil. That and fish crumbs were right up there among my favourite snacks.

One afternoon, as I headed home with my brown school case and a sweet I had specially saved up for and was not going to eat until I had swanked with it first in front of my friend Levi, I bumped into a ruffian. Actually, this sweet – which cost five cents – took me weeks to save up for. It was hugely indulgent, given the amount of food I could have bought with the money. What fascinated me about this particular sweet was that it was moulded in the form of a flute. You could actually blow it like an instrument and when you were tired of doing that, you could just eat it.

I was excited as I walked home that afternoon. I did not even see the bully who was waiting at the other end of the passage. Before I knew it, he was on me, searching me for any money I might have in my possession. He roughed me up a little around the shoulders and face and then produced an okapi knife, a switchblade with a mahogany handle and a sharp blade of ten to fifteen centimetre.

"Open the bloody suitcase," he bellowed at me after realising that I had locked it.

I looked into his cold eyes and at the knife in his hand and decided that the sweet could go. His name was Geelboy and he belonged to a gang called Madamara. I had heard stories about him before. Although his build was relatively slight, he had a reputation for knifing people at will, irrespective of their age. After I had opened the case for him, he threw my books onto the ground and my sweet fell out.

"Voetsek, vaya, son!" He chased me away as he inspected the sweet.

I quickly picked up all my books and ran away. As I walked towards my house I felt the tears rolling down my cheeks.

Of course I made a point of wiping away my tears well before I reached home.

Shortly after that incident, when Gilbert, Lesego and Pontsho suggested that we gazaat – club together – for lunch, I was more than a willing partner because the plan would save me from being robbed of my school money by bullies. Even though the four of us attended two different schools and were at those schools at three different times, we managed to work out a scheme whereby those at lower primary school, Pontsho and myself, would go to meet Gilbert and Lesego at their higher primary school, which took its lunch-break at two o'clock. Because their lunch was only fifteen minutes long, Gilbert and Lesego had to eat as fast as they could. As to myself and Pontsho, we just had to grab our share and be off as we were not allowed to be on the premises of another school after lunch-break. However, since Lesego was entrusted with buying the food, it also meant that Pontsho and I did not eat during our normal lunch-breaks, which were at eleven and one o'clock, depending on whether we were attending morning or afternoon classes. But no matter the sacrifices, that arrangement surely saved me from being robbed of my school allowance for some time to come.

Lower Primary

One of my chores during the week was to build the fire in our coal stove. I was nine then, in Standard One. Because I was the youngest, I was also the first home in the afternoons. This meant that next to the responsibility of making the fire, I also had the responsibility of walking around with the house key, a situation which presented countless opportunities for mischief. With Levi and myself around, creativity in the rascal department was easy to come by; it was our forte.

I remember the day we dismantled my brother's tape recorder and failed to reassemble it. That day, as the time approached when Moropa would come home, I played as far away from the house as I could. I swore on my great-grandfather's grave that I knew nothing about the tape recorder. I swore that I did not even know he had it, even though we had taped my voice just the day before. And I got away with it.

Many times Levi and I scraped the condensed milk container clean and then swore to my mother that we had not even been in the house. Gold Cross condensed milk was irresistible, but it came with a disturbing legacy attached to it.

There was a time in Diepkloof, if not in the whole of Soweto, when almost all primary school children were on the hunt for Gold Cross labels. If your school collected a certain number, the makers of Gold Cross condensed milk would reward the school with soccer gear for the boys and netball gear for the girls. As a result, every school expected their pupils to gather as many labels as they could, but at least around twenty per pupil, within the given time. At home we used one can of Gold Cross a week, which translated into a mere four labels a month. As a result we, the primary school children in the house, had to go to dumping sites looking for labels. The biggest dumping site was in Zone Six, which was just opposite the present-day Chris Hani Baragwanath Hospital. That was one hell of a long and dangerous walk for small boys like myself.

Moving from Zone Four through Zone Five did not present much of a problem at that time because there was joint patronage between the two areas, since the feared Madamara gang had members living in both zones. The leader of the gang was Mandla-Sandlana, and he lived in Zone Five.

The major problem was Zone Six. What sent shivers down my spine whenever I thought about Zone Six was the story I had been told by a boy named Seun ... that was his name, Seun.

Seun lived in Zone Five, where my aunt and uncle rented a room in Seun's parents' house. Seun told me that a group of boys once attempted to slaughter him with a piece of rusted iron, just like the elders would slaughter a cow or goat or sheep. He told me that the gang had him pinned spread-eagled on the ground and were working on his throat when he managed to slip free and run for his life. If they could do that to a boy who lived in Zone Five, whose house was separated by a mere street from Zone Six, then imagine what they could do to me, a "foreigner" from Zone Four. I didn't even know the Zulu language, which was a dangerous weakness around Zone Six as well as Zone Two and parts of Zone One. These areas were dominated by Zulu-speaking people who had little or no respect for people who could not speak their language. As a "foreigner", you risked life and limb crossing these territories.

As for Levi and myself, using our craftiness and street cunning, we managed to survive the few weeks of the Gold Cross torture. But it wasn't a time, with all the running and diving we had to do to collect the Gold Cross labels, that we would easily forget. Yet I can't even remember if our school won any soccer or netball gear out of the whole indaba.

Levi and I were friends from our days at crèche. When we first met, my family lived on the western side of Zone Four and Levi's family lived on the eastern side. However, when later we moved house to the eastern side, I found myself living three houses away from Levi. It was just unbelievable that we had moved so close to my crèche buddy. Having Levi so nearby made me forget all my old friends back where we came from, and cemented our friendship. That Levi was nearly two years younger than me and that we spoke different languages at home made no difference to us. We just got on so well.

Levi was always the first one to arrive at my place in the morning, and sometimes he was the last person I saw at the end of the day. Later, when we were both finally at primary school – because

My childhood home in Zone 4, where I found myself living three houses away from my best friend, Levi.

The crèche where I grew to hate butter beans.

of his age, he started primary school later than I did – I was envious of the fact that he could go to the school just opposite my house while I had to walk a long distance to my school. Primary schools were organised according to language groups, and since Levi was Mosotho and I was Motswana we could not go to the same school.

It was not only the distance that bothered me. I would have loved to have gone to the same school as my crèche buddy because of the happiness I got out of being around Levi.

Not that I ever particularly enjoyed my time at crèche. In fact, to be frank, I hated crèche. The first thing I hated about crèche was beans ... butter beans. Every day at lunch-time we ate either samp with butter beans or soup with butter beans. Can you imagine having to put up with such a diet for four years? And yes ... let me not forget the soft porridge every morning and the slice of brown bread with jam at knock-off time. The person responsible for that kind of diet, I think, could do with a long spell or two in boarding school or even prison. I ate beans to the point where I loathed them – loathed them so much that when they cooked samp at home with beans, they had to cook mine separately without the beans. And when they cooked soup with beans, I had to be served something else.

The other reason why I hated crèche was this boy Bryan. Bryan was a little boy with a cute face whose mother, it was said, was a close friend of the teacher's, if not a relative. Bryan was the bright boy in crèche, but what really made me angry was that he was simply untouchable. The teacher's protection made Bryan powerful.

After lunch, whether we liked it or not, we all had to sleep, except for Bryan. While we were ordered to sleep, the teacher would hand him a piece of wood from a tomato box. Bryan's job was to punish those who did not close their eyes or keep still. I am one of those people who sleeps with his eyes half open. At crèche, I always managed to squeeze them tightly shut before I fell asleep, but can you imagine what used to happen when I was fast asleep and the "golden boy" strolled passed me? He would lash out at my buttocks with his piece of wood, screaming that I was not asleep.

Day after day I went to sleep in that crèche knowing that I was going to be punished for no reason, and there was absolutely nothing I could do about it. I could not even tell my mother about it – she would have simply dismissed it as an excuse for not wanting to go to crèche. This would have been especially so if I complained when schools were on their ten-day Easter holidays, which were not applicable to kids at crèche. I just could not understand why all of my school-going brothers and sisters should get to stay at home and do what they like while I had to go to crèche. I sighed with relief when, in 1971, I finally graduated to lower primary school.

But, once I arrived at Ikaneng Lower Primary School, things were not as rosy as I had anticipated. The first day, all the newcomers from various crèches were crammed into one classroom. Some were crying and some even wet themselves.

If this was what school was all about, maybe it was better to go and challenge Bryan at crèche. I looked around and saw him standing there, as distressed and confused as everyone else, and suddenly I felt a little better. Anything that made Bryan miserable was good for me. Maybe I would have the opportunity to get even with Bryan at school, I thought.

But as the days passed I realised that was not to be. At school I found myself confronted with another version of Bryan in the form of Nhlanhla. Nhlanhla was repeating Sub A. Whenever the teacher left the classroom, she left Nhlanhla in charge, to watch over those who made a noise or strayed from their "desks" – which were not real desks but narrow bunks meant for seating. We had to kneel next to these "desks" when it was time to write.

Remarkably, the teacher put up with a fair bit of noise from us, but when she left the classroom and the veteran Nhlanhla was playing policeman, the rules of the game in the class changed. With Nhlanhla, silence meant silence. If I happened to sneeze, I found myself in trouble, because sneezing could not be done quietly. According to Nhlanhla's rule book, sneezing was regarded as making a noise. Even yawning was a violation.

According to the policy of the classroom, Nhlanhla was supposed to pull anyone who made a noise to the front of the class. The unfortunate ones would have to stand in a row in front of the class, next to the chalkboard, and await their punishment. In order for Nhlanhla to be convinced that you were quiet, you had to place your forefinger across your lips as a sign that your lips were locked together. There was one girl, Mmapitso, who understood things differently. She would deliberately speak with her forefinger over her lips. And when Nhlanhla wanted to pull her up to the front of the class, she would cling to the bench like a leach. Nhlanhla would pull harder, trying to move her and her bench. Sometimes Mmapitso would bite Nhlanhla's hands to disentangle herself. This actually made things worse for her. It was like resisting arrest or assaulting a policeman. Nhlanhla would scream out angrily and later report her to the teacher.

Mmapitso would regularly get extra lashes, yet she repeated this behaviour and resistance almost every day. For her, silence was like a curse.

Apart from Nhlanhla there was another problem I faced: covers … the protective plastic covers that went over exercise books. I could not understand why, but I always misplaced the outside covers. Midway through the year, I had only one cover left for all my exercise books. This meant I had to swap the cover from book to book each time we had to hand in a book so that our teacher – known to us as "Mistress" – could take it home for marking.

How our female teachers came to be known to us as "Mistress" I could never quite fathom. On top of that, the word mistress became shortened for convenience. According to township street protocol, conventional nouns were less colourful and less vibrant than our township lingo and rhymes. We formulated words with a better township "rhythm and flow". So, for example, mistress became miza, teacher became tiza or simply "T", and principal became prinzi.

The only consolation about being at lower primary was the fact that the principal knew me as the younger sibling of my brother, Gilbert, and my sisters, Pontsho and Lesego, who had gone to the school before me. The principal had obviously liked them. But despite this advantage, I was wary of the principal, because of her whip. Prinzi was well known at school for her whip, which was like an extension of her arm. She did not use a cane, made of bamboo or wood, like most teachers, but preferred this whip, a leather sjambok. Whenever she saw me, she would call me aside so that she could ask questions about my brother and sisters, especially Gilbert, but also about my parents. As she spoke to me, she would gently swing the whip across my feet. The tip of the whip, despite the gentleness of her swing, would nevertheless do its job. She would swish it from one side to the other, and as it swung it would sting the tops of my bare feet. I would answer her questions twitching madly, trying to block the whip every time it swung towards my feet.

I vividly remember her large white smile that seemed to stand out like false teeth beneath the big wig she always wore on her head. It was this wig which prompted a debate among us little boys about her racial origins.

"Prinzi ya rone ke lekgowa," is how we used to tell our friends from different schools that "our principal is a white woman".

"If she is white how can she speak Setswana?" was the logical question that followed from our friends. "And why is she not living in town, but in Orlando?" was another logical question.

That she lived in Orlando did not mean much to me. The only thing I knew about Orlando was that it had a famous soccer stadium, where we gathered once or twice a year for athletics. I also knew that in Orlando you had to speak Zulu, even if you did not know the language; you also had to say you were a fan of Orlando Pirates, even if you were not. According to my friends and me, Prinzi's brown wigs and unusually light complexion, which was always painted in heavy make-up, was more than enough to qualify her as a white woman, irrespective of where she lived or what language she spoke. The greeting she made famous at the school still rings in my ears. "Dear bana" – children – she used to say, and we had to reply, "Dear Hosie!" To this day I still have not figured out what Hosie meant.

I was not sure whether she enjoyed whipping my bare feet in some sort of sadistic way, or if it was just a genuine eccentricity and she did not realise what she was doing as she swung her whip gently to and fro. She was a bit like a teacher we had been told about at higher primary school who punished boys just for the fun of it. It was said that this teacher would call a boy, give him a lashing, and when the boy asked what it was for, the teacher would reply: "You are a boy, you must have done something wrong at one stage or another and got away with it. Or, if you have not done anything wrong, no doubt you are going to do something wrong in the future. In which case, I am punishing you in advance. Now, go away."

One thing I understood was that if Nana Pooe – that was Prinzi's real name – caught me without a tie, she would punish me. According to Prinzi a tie was the most important part of the school uniform. Even if you came to school wearing the school's official cap, blazer, jersey, shorts and socks but no tie, you would be in trouble. Usually I wore black short pants and a white shirt with a multi-coloured, non-regulation school tie, but as long as I had a tie on I was a good boy. I must say, though, that for a long time I did not do well in the tie department. In the beginning, it seemed to me that it was only when I saw Prinzi that I remembered my tie. And since she knew me and was fond of having conversations with me, there was little chance of avoiding her. Finally, I formulated a simple rule for not forgetting my tie. I counted the items of clothing that I wore to school. If, when I was dressed and ready, they were fewer than three, then I knew I had forgotten something. The items of clothing I always wore, and which were mandatory, were short pants, white shirt, and tie. The others, like a blazer, cap, even shoes and jerseys, which I had inherited plenty of from my brothers and sisters, were just cumbersome to me. In most cases I had to be threatened before I would wear any of these items to school, especially shoes and a jersey. "If you come back and cough all night," my mother would threaten, "then you will go and sleep in the toilet."

Despite problems with book covers and ties, I must say I also had moments of glory at Ikaneng. One day I was instructed by my Sub B teacher to go to the office and ask the principal to open my Setswana book at any page, and let me read to her from it. Prinzi was so impressed with my performance that she took me from one class to the other, asking the different teachers to do the same. I read every page they chose that day, loudly and clearly. I watched Bryan's face when I was standing in front of his class. I felt like telling him, "This is not crèche, mfana – boy – this is school. And today I am the man and you can eat your heart out."

Another glorious moment came at the end of Standard Two, when, after a long struggle with Clothilda, I managed to come first in class. That's right, that was her name ... Clothilda. I have never ever met anyone else by that name in all my years. Due to a strange coincidence, Clothilda's father was my distant relative. To make matters worse, I had the same Setswana name as her father.

I was afraid of Clothilda, mentally as well as physically. She was smart, and she did not hesitate to give any boy who started with her a hard slap across the face. One slap from her and tears would roll down the offending boy's cheeks. End of story.

The other contender for the number one position in class was a boy called Elijah. But fortunately for Clothilda, he had dropped out of school by Standard One, and from then on it was Clothilda who came first in everything.

There was something strange about Elijah, related to his hair. The curls of his hair were bigger than ours, and his hair was black and shiny just like that of coloured people. Maybe that was why miza liked him. But I think the main reason was that he was light on his feet. He had the shortest turn-around time of anyone when he was sent to buy lunch for the teacher. And, of course, he was also the genius of the class. What we could not understand was the fact that he left school. I mean, someone like him, who was the brains of the class!

I did not like school-dodgers, not because of them skipping school, but for the simple reason that they gave boys like me extra work. By "boys like me" I mean boys who were regarded as the big boys in the class because of their height. We were the ones who were sent to track down school-dodgers and told not to return until we had nabbed the culprits. When we returned, we were expected to hold the offenders upside down so that the teacher could cane their buttocks.

The worst was that school-dodgers made us appear bad, because we were the ones sent out to find them. Their loathing for us extended beyond the school fence and we ended up having unnecessary foes, some of them living in strategic positions, like Mongesi who lived next door to dishipa – the shops. For someone like me who had to go to the shops almost every day for fresh milk or bread, that was a nightmare. I had to be as swift as a cheetah on my feet and as quick as an eagle with my eyes to avoid running into Mongesi and the inevitable beating he would give me.

As you can imagine, chasing after a school-dodger could easily turn ugly, and sometimes the hunter even turned into the hunted.

This was what happened with Elijah the last time we went after him. Elijah was a glue-sniffer and he and his glue-sniffing friends laid an ambush for us. We spotted Elijah sitting comfortably on top of the remains of a burnt-out car next to the rubbish dump, not far away from the shops. What surprised me with school-dodgers was that we always found them in school uniform. I was glad to see Elijah on that day. At least we did not have to run all over the place to find him – for me running was a big no-no, which I avoided whenever I could. I did not have the chest or the stamina for it.

When we closed in on Elijah, the leader of our troop said, as was always said: "Miza said we must come and fetch you." Before he could say another word, stones came flying at us from all directions. We turned and fled. At first we tried to gather stones as we ran, to retaliate, but we quickly realised that the opposition was too well prepared for us. What saved us was that one boy from our group suffered an injury to the forehead. It looked so bad, with blood streaming down his face, that our attackers ran away in fright. We ran back to school to get help for the injured boy and to show the teacher what Elijah and his glue-sniffing friends had done to us.

Though no one was keen to be sent after school-dodgers, this duty still fell on us from time to time. But at least Elijah was left alone after that incident.

Standard Two, with no competition from Elijah, was Clothilda's year. Not only was she bright and had the courage to give a boy a good clap if he deserved it, she was also good at sports – and she was cute, which probably explained why the boys were keen to get so close to her. But that day, at the end of the school year, it was announced that I had taken over the number one position in the class. I looked at Clothilda's disappointed face and felt like saying, "You are going to clap me for this, too? Just try it." Of course I never said anything.

Levi and I

Levi had enemies everywhere ... and most of them were older than him. The fact that he did not have a big brother might have exacerbated the state of affairs. To make matters even worse, he had two older sisters and a younger sister. One of his sisters was, of course, Nokuthula. Since the day of the hanky-panky, she and I never saw eye to eye. An animosity developed between us and we became rivals. Whenever we met, sparks flew. We fought each other openly, and physically. I remember one day she attacked me with her nails, clinching them into me as though she were ready to tear my face apart. I had to throw all sorts of flying kicks and punches to keep her at bay. Such scenes became common while my friendship with Levi lasted.

Although nearly two years younger than me, it was Levi who introduced me to the streets as well as to the night. I was terrified of darkness, especially in Diepkloof, where there was very little electricity. There were some street lights in the neighbourhood, but they were seldom in working condition, not so much because the mmasepala – municipality – did not care, but mainly because we kids derived so much pleasure from stoning the street lights to smithereens. The attitude that reigned in the township in those days was, "After all, these things do not belong to us, they belong to mmasepala." The same went for school windows. I remember how we used to use school windows for target practice. It was a case of, "Let's see who can hit the window from here." We would stand up to fifty metres away and throw stones like they were bullets from a machine gun. There was victory in the sound of a window collapsing under the force of your stone. From a pragmatic point of view, these target practices were necessary because we needed to be crack-sharp with stones to defend ourselves in the more than occasional street fights we found ourselves embroiled in.

Back to the darkness. I did not like darkness because it made me feel scared and insecure. The things that happened in the dark were brutal. People were murdered at night only to be found dead on some road or in some field the next morning. There was a time in Zone Four when corpses appeared every Saturday morning, to a point where we knew that women sitting next to a bundle covered in newspapers, meant that death had passed.

But around Levi, I forgot all about my fear of darkness. We played all day long, and after sunset we used to make thezi – fire. For one to be granted permission to stand with us around our thezi, one had to go votha – collect materials to keep the fire burning. This, in a sense, helped to keep our environment clean from papers. We burnt everything we could lay our hands on. We were, however, cautious when it came to chachas – burning plastic. We understood the dangers of burning plastic from experience. Levi, for one, bore a scar on his foot, which was left by chachas. I was also left with a scar at the back of my calf as a result of chachas. We would sit around the fire until eight at night or later, when my sister would come to get me. We normally made thezi adjacent to the school fence, which was just metres away from my home.

The older boys told me that I was a fool and was never going to grow wise if I remained afraid of the darkness. They said that they played black maipatile – hide and seek – at night, and claimed it was much more rewarding than the same game played in the day. I could not understand the difference between the two black maipatiles. They said it was because they played with girls. We also played with girls during the day. "You are stupid," they said. It took me years to understand what they meant.

My daring in the dark went as far as standing around the thezi next door to my house. Beyond that, darkness was a big *not on your life*. Because she knew how terrified I was of the dark, my mother used to threaten me with locking me up in the outside toilet at night.

"The problem with you is that you haven't looked after cattle in the rural areas," my father used to say. "When we were growing up, we used to wake up at about four in the morning to take the cattle out to graze before we went to school. We would then go and pick them up in the afternoon after school. I remember one day I lost some of my father's cattle. I was made to go and look for them in the middle of the night. That night, young and alone as I was, I actually slept in the bush. And you are afraid of the dark here in the township! Maybe I should take you to the rural areas for a year so that they can teach you to become brave."

After that story, I used to look at my father and think, brave – yes, that would be nice; rural areas – not until hell freezes over.

But for Levi it was a different story; nothing seemed to scare him, especially not the dark, and as if to prove it we found him sleeping outside, in our toilet, very late one night. I think it might already have been early morning when we found him there. I had heard stories about things that happened late at night. At one time I heard people talking of a gorilla that moved about in the dark with a chain and if you crossed its path you would be killed. We sometimes heard heavy, slow movements up and down our street at night and the next morning all the kids in the street would be talking about how they tried to peep out of their windows but could not see what was causing the eerie sounds. And then there was the sound of howling dogs that sometimes went on right through the night. We also often heard the meows of cats, like children crying in the night, and we would wonder if they were really cats ...

With these thoughts in my mind, I tried to imagine a boy, not even eight, sleeping in an outside toilet in the dark, all by himself. It made me shudder. This outside toilet in Diepkloof was a tiny structure of one meter by one and a half meter. The door did not even cover the whole doorway; it was a full twenty-five centimetres short at the top and bottom ends. As far as I was concerned, that door provided no security against any of a hundred beasts which could have attacked Levi that night.

I valued the security of my home, the warmth and the comfort, and could not see myself sleeping in an outside toilet. As the last-born at home, I was the most protected member of the family. "O tlogele ngwana wa ko gae ... o mo tlogele" – You just leave my little brother alone! – was the way my sisters used to come to my rescue at times, with aggressive pride and protectiveness in their stance.

"You don't do that with my laetie" – my little brother – were the words my brothers used to give stern warning to anyone who tried to be nasty with me. "I don't want to hear anything more about my gofetjane – last-born – do you hear me?" was how my mother came to my aid during sibling squabbles, wagging her finger at my older brothers and sisters. "This is my last-born," my father would say and hug me around my shoulders as he introduced me to his friends.

It was this warmth and security I enjoyed at home that really made me wonder what compelled Levi to run away from home that night and choose our toilet as a shelter.

The day Levi was found in the toilet, my parents decided to take him in for the night. My mother prepared a bed for him in the kitchen. The following morning we woke up and brushed our teeth together and had tea together. I was so happy to be able to do that with Levi. I felt like asking my folks if it was okay for Levi to come and stay with us on a permanent basis. After tea, my mother said to Levi, "Come, let's go and see your parents," and off she went with Levi. "Where do you think you are going," she stopped me from following them. There was something in her voice and the way she looked at me that made me realise that what was happening was more than I could comprehend. But my mother never ever told me about what Levi or his parents said about the incident. Levi, too, never mentioned anything about the incident to me, and for some reason I did not feel free to ask. I simply continued to see him as brave and fearless for spending an entire night alone outside in the haunting dark.

It has to be said that I had stuck my neck out on several occasions for Levi. In most cases I was able to negotiate a way out of the scraps he managed to get himself into with his multitude of adversaries. "I am so sorry, my brother," I would plead with head bent slightly to one side while my hands would be clasped together in front of my chest. "I can assure you that he will never do something like this again." In most cases it worked, but there were times when it did not work.

"Is he your laetie?" the angry bigger boy would ask me.

"No, he is my friend," I would reply in a submissive manner.

"Then why are you protecting him?"

"Because he is my friend and I ..."

"In that case I will have to punish both of you," the older boy would retort, and whatever punishment was dished out to Levi was also dished out to me. At this point, we tried to break free and run for our lives.

In the course of the many negotiations I handled on Levi's behalf, I sometimes had to make promises to older boys which, in the end, were difficult to keep. Once, to protect Levi from a sure beating, I promised to give a boy five cents the next day if he would let go of Levi. I don't know what got into me because five cents was a lot of money. Days went by and I completely forgot about that promise until I met Willie again.

"Where is my money?" Willie demanded when I bumped into him on my way back from the shops one day. "You promised to give it to me the next day and I am still waiting, sonny." I could see in his eyes that he was not impressed with my breaking the promise. The use of the word "sonny" indicated his contempt. He saw me as a little boy compared to himself.

"I do not have it now," I said turning my pockets inside out. "But I will give it to you tomorrow."

"If I do not get it by tomorrow, ke tlo go roba – I am going to break you – sonny," he threatened, shoving his finger into my forehead and pushing me backwards.

Now that Willie had laid his cards on the table, I had to be careful about my movements. "If Willie truly thinks I'm going to give him my whole daily allowance just like that, then he has another thing coming," I said bravely to myself. I planned to avoid Willie from that day on. What made this difficult was that I had to pass by his house every time I went to the shops. To avoid him, I ended up walking a fair way eastwards and then cutting back to the shops which were in the opposite direction, due south west of my house.

After ducking and diving for a few days, Willie eventually caught sight of me coming out of the shops and chased me all the way home.

"What's wrong, boy?" my mother asked him as he stood at the kitchen door, breathing just as heavily as I was, where I was safely leaning against the kitchen table.

"Alex owes me five cents and he does not want to pay me back," he replied rasping for air.

My mother turned to me, "Is that so?" She looked at me in a way that said you better tell me the truth or else ...

I could have said no and my mother would have chased Willie away, but I decided to keep quiet. After all, I had to think long-term. A "no" meant a multiplication of the antagonism between Willie and myself. A "yes" meant retribution from my mother as she had warned me on several occasions, "I do not want a child who walks around borrowing money as if we do not give him enough here at home." So, given the odds, silence represented a kind of break-even point.

"I want you to give him his money now," my mother said, as she pinched my ear.

"Mmaaa!" I cried out, reaching for my mother's hand, but her fingers were digging tightly into my ear. "I do not have it now. *Ijooo!* I will give it to him tomorrow."

After the pinching was over and I was wiping the tears from my face, I realised that Willie was laughing all the way out of the yard. I thought to myself, if he thinks that will make me give him my five cents, then he is in for a big surprise. As far as I was concerned, I had already been punished. The next day came and I did not give Willie his money. It felt good.

One afternoon, a few days later, as I was on my way home from school, I saw a group of boys gathered in the street not far away from the school. I approached cautiously. They had formed a ring and in the centre of the ring were three boys. One of them was Willie. In the middle, standing slightly back from Willie and the other boy, stood a boy with both his hands stretched out towards Willie and the other boy. He had a heap of soil in each hand. I knew what that meant. It meant a challenge for a fia-go or fia-fia – township slang for "fair fist-fight". The boy in the middle with the hands full of soil was the referee, and the boy making the challenge would have to slap the soil from the one hand, and then his opponent would either accept the challenge by slapping the soil from the other hand or decline by refusing to take the handful of soil. Refusing a challenge was branded legwala – from the Zulu word "igwala" meaning coward. It was better to be beaten in a fair fight than to be branded legwala, because, from then on, it would be broadcast through the length and breadth of your community that you were afraid to face up to fia-go. The rules of fia-go were simple: no biting, kicking or stoning. In most cases, these rules were observed by the stronger party and ignored by the losing party. I had seen some bad losers in fia-fia who, almost from the beginning of the fight, had resorted to all of the above. In this particular fight Willie was taking on a boy who was bigger than him. The heaps of soil were accepted by both boys, and I gleefully expected to see Willie get the hiding I thought he deserved.

The two fighters started to warm up and the bigger boy, as if to show his prowess, shouted, "Wait!" He took off his shirt and licked his fists with his tongue. He then dipped his fists into the loose soil at his feet. I had heard it said that a punch with granules of soil on the fist was extremely painful, though, to be honest, I was not quite sure who for. In this instance, it looked like the bigger boy aimed to do some serious damage to Willie.

The fight began and the two boys started throwing punches, some missing and some landing haphazardly. Then, out of the blue, with lightning speed, Willie landed a crushing blow on the bigger boy's nose and blood started gushing out. The bigger boy looked at the blood after feeling his nose with his hand and looked at Willie with eyes on fire. But it did not help him. Willie came back stronger than before and landed a torrent of blows all over the bigger boy's head and body.

After a couple of minutes of this punishment the bigger boy began to cry and started to look around for stones. That's when I saw how good Willie was at street fighting. As the bigger boy started hurling stones, Willie managed to skip and jump out of the way of all of them, then he picked up one large stone for himself and threw it hard at his cowardly opponent. Only Willie's stone did not miss but hit the bigger boy in the ribs. The bigger boy turned and ran away crying.

I, too, withdrew slowly from the crowd and disappeared. That was the day I decided I was going to pay Willie the money I had promised him. The next day, on my way to school, I passed by his house and gave him his money. There was no way I wanted to see myself in the same position as that poor big boy.

On one occasion involving Levi, I had to stand by helplessly and watch Pitso hold Levi upside down, trying to force him to eat dog shit from the pavement. This, of course, was in the days before Pitso became Nokuthula's boyfriend and he and Levi ended up great buddies with Levi getting into Bra Hohle's movies for free. Levi's mouth was so close to the shit that I thought he was going to have to eat it. Levi and I were heavily outnumbered that day. When we were cornered by Pitso and his gang, there were seven of them and just the two of us.

"You stay out of this if you do not want to end up like him," one of Pitso's friends warned me as I was about to engage in negotiations. "You have no idea what this gamors – rubbish – has done to us."

Levi, as the only boy in his family, frequently had to put up fights in defence of his sisters. This explained why most of his enemies were Nokuthula's age – which was about my age – or older. Levi, as already intimated, also had to suffer the consequences of not having a big brother.

The status of one's brother could either save or destroy one. The normal question was: "O ntwana ya mang?" – Whose little brother are you? If you mentioned a name which they did not know or for whom they had no regard, they would simply go ahead and beat you up. I had four brothers, and unfortunately none of their names sent shivers across the streets. As a result, I was almost in the same predicament as Levi, who was without older brothers.

I remember an incident at school when I was in Sub A. The inspector was due to visit the school and the day before his visit we had to give the school a thorough cleaning. Our class was assigned to picking up papers and clearing out the weeds in the rows of grass between the classrooms. Somehow I ended up side-tracked from the group and back in our classroom.

Inside the class were a group of older boys who were helping one of the teachers with some touch-up painting to the walls. I walked into the class and immediately the teacher asked why I was not with my group. Failing to give an adequate explanation, the teacher asked, "Do you know him, boys?"

The boys looked at one another and shook their heads. One of them asked the others, "Ke ntwana ya mang?" – Whose little brother is he? The heads continued shaking.

"Who are your brothers?" one of the boys then asked me directly, and I told them my brothers' names. Still the heads shook. It seemed, in my case, having older brothers made not an iota of difference.

"Come here," the teacher now called angrily to me. She picked up a cane from the desk and lashed me on the backside. Then, as if that lashing were not enough, she made me go and pick one hundred blades of grass for her. At that age I could only count up to twenty-nine. So when I had gathered twenty-nine blades of grass, I counted twenty-ten, twenty-eleven and continued to count until I had reached twenty-twenty-nine. From there I started with twenty-twenty-nine-one, and so it went on. I can't remember where the counting ended, only that the teacher was satisfied with the handful of grass I finally handed over to her.

Back to Levi, Pitso and the shit on the sidewalk.

"Do you swear that you will never do it again?" Pitso asked Levi, still holding him upside down while I looked on helplessly.

"Ma vra wao wao," Levi swore as tears swelled out of his eyes. "I will never do it again."

I wanted to step in and ask exactly what it was that Levi had done to deserve this punishment when Pitso let Levi fall to the ground, just centimetres away from the dog shit.

"Next time," Pitso wagged a finger at Levi, who was wiping his mouth with the back of his hand, "I'll make you eat all the shit along this street."

"Don't worry, we will get him one day," I consoled Levi, who was still crying as Pitso and his bunch of bullies left the area.

"I am defenceless against these guys," Levi said between sobs. "They will come back and do the same thing again, and there is nothing I can do about it."

"Do not worry, my friend, one day is one day." I just shook my head feeling the pain in Levi's voice but still none the wiser as to why Pitso and his friends were picking on him. It was not too long, anyway, before he and Pitso would be the best of friends.

Work and play

For me, playing was the reason for living. Anything that violated my right to play, I simply loathed. And one of the main things violating my right to play was church. I was forced to go to church. I could not see why I had to leave my friends at great games while I had to go to church. I did not see any attraction or excitement in going to church. Church, according to my reckoning, should have been abolished. It was dead boring. But I did not have any choice, as my parents insisted, and all my brothers and sisters went to church. "How will you be able to get your Dedication and Baptism papers?" my mother would ask me. "In fact, I should talk to Father Maleka ... I want you to be one of the servers." I did not understand what my mother saw in being an altar boy. I did not see any fun in it. Maybe it was the fact that Lesego was a member of the church choir and Pontsho was a member of the St Agnes guild that made her think I should follow in their footsteps.

I always watched the altar boys as they made their rounds through the church. The only one who really interested me was the leading altar boy who walked around with something that looked like a steel weapon from mediaeval times and made a lot of smoke. The way he swung the hexagonal ball-like thing on its silver chain, reminded me of some of the kung fu movies I was in awe of. Maybe

I should try for that, I thought. But on finding out how many altar boys were in line for the leading position, I decided it was not even worth the try. After that, to my mother's dismay, I dropped all interest in the altar boy thing.

"But why should I have those papers?" I used to ask my mother about the Dedication and Baptism papers she was always mouthing on about.

"Those papers will be necessary when you apply for your pass," my mother explained, referring to the apartheid identification document used to monitor the movements of blacks.

Knowing that people caught without passes always ended up in the back of the kwela-kwela, the big ugly-looking police vans that everyone in the townships hated, I obliged.

Another thing I detested about church was the Sunday clothes I had to wear. These clothes were a massive limitation on my ability to play. In the long trousers and jacket I had to wear, I did not feel free to do the things I was able to do in my short pants and short-sleeved shirt. Every Sunday, as soon as I could, I would run back home after church and change into my normal play clothes. This resulted in most of my church clothes being given away as new, because I outgrew them hardly ever having worn them.

I grudgingly attended church services at St James Anglican Church (Zone 3, Diepkloof), the white building in the background.

Working was contrary to my beliefs. I held the view that doing chores around the house was girls' work, especially having two older sisters around. My mother worked hard to change my view. "O a gafa. O ithaya gore o ya go nyokotla fela mo gae," – You are out of your mind if you think you are only going to gobble around the house without lifting a finger – she would remonstrate.

I just could not bring myself to understand the idea of working around the house at my age. I saw myself as a little person who did not qualify to lift even a feather around the house. And remember, of course, I was also "last-born", which I believed placed me in a privileged position.

But I often forgot my loathing for work when I was on my way to school in the mornings, especially on those days when we were supposed to have memorised verses from the Bible or poetry for oral recitation. At these times I would look up at the Soweto freeway and gaze jealously at all the cars driving bumper to bumper. I used to ask myself whether the workers in those cars and buses were ever confronted with speculation that they were going to be punished on a particular day because they had not done their homework. I concluded that since they did not have any homework, there was no way they could be anything but happy to be going to work. Plus, they were even paid for going to work. I dreamt of the day when I would be finished with school and punishment and driving to work in my own Dodge Monaco, or Six Mabone – six lights – as we used to call them because of the number of their tail lights. Or maybe I could even be like Caiphus's uncle, driving my own taxi? Caiphus's uncle drove a white Valiant Regal, a Valaza, as we used to call them, and he inspired awe among us boys. Then again, I would even settle for driving the Bedford Mangulungulu – from the Zulu word khulu meaning "big" – that Spete's father drove, rather than be at school and face punishment,

Spete lived two houses away from us and his father was a man with a big heart. Every day upon his return home from work, he would stop outside my house and all the children, especially us boys, would be encouraged to jump onto the back of his big green truck. Even though it was a drive of less than fifty metres to his home, it was a great thrill for all of us.

But back to Caiphus. I used to look up to Caiphus with envy as he showed me the handful of silver coins he had salvaged from the back seat of his uncle's Valiant Regal taxi. I was puzzled when he told me, "The back seat searches the passengers for me." I just could not imagine a car seat producing two hands and roughing the passengers up like bullies used to do with us, and shaking them out for money. But that did not concern me as much as the benefits Caiphus enjoyed from that inexplicable occurrence.

It was much the same bewilderment that I had inside my head about the big red cylindrical box outside the Post Office, which was located at Diepkloof Zone One ya maZulu – Zone One for Zulus. Zone One had two divisions, the Zulu and the Sotho divisions. It also had two shopping facilities, one for Zulus and the other for Sothos. The Zulu facility was opposite the Diepkloof soccer fields and the beer hall.

What worried me was how it was possible that by placing an envelope in that round red thing it would end up on the other side of the country. I asked my friends and all they told me was, "You will never understand the ways of the white men ... those people are very clever."

How I sometimes wished Caiphus would call for my help when he was asked to wash his uncle's taxi. The only money I ever laid my hands on was the five cents school allowance my father gave me. Money was rarely available for other things.

I was not like Jimmy, who always had loads of money to spend. Jimmy lived a few houses up the street, and according to Levi, Thabang and me, he came from a rich family. There were a few indicators which brought us to this conclusion. Their four-roomed house, though the standard Soweto size, was plastered on the outside and the standard windows were replaced with bigger windows. Also, Jimmy had a bicycle, the dream of every township boy.

Since I started school, each year I was promised that if I passed at the end of the year, I would get a bicycle. But even the year I came first in class I never received my bicycle.

Jimmy, having a bicycle as well as a seemingly unending money supply, was in a position that elevated him above us all. He could buy a plastic soccer ball any time he wanted. You know what that meant? That meant he could form his own soccer team any time he wanted and have complete control over it, which was exactly what he did. He had the power to invite players as well as the power to drop a player even in the middle of a game. He was manager, coach and captain of his club. Without him there was no club; without him there could be no match. Whatever he suggested was law, it was his way or the highway. If the agreement between two soccer teams was change two drop four, and he decided change five drop ten, so it would be. "Change and drop" was a mechanism developed by us small boys to "time" matches because we did not have watches. "Change and drop" meant, say, in the case of a change five drop ten game, that if a team scored five goals that was halftime, irrespective of the duration; when ten goals were scored by one team, it was the end of the game. As a result, some soccer games took fifteen minutes while others took almost half a day.

In the main, given the limited resources available in our communities, it was better to hang around people like Jimmy, who had resources, than risk going to the playgrounds. Playgrounds belonged to the bullies who lived in those areas. Us little ones, who had walked all the way to a playground, had to play with one eye on the see-saw and the other on the road, because if the bullies found us there, there would be no mercy and we would get beaten. The other thing was that our parents often warned us not to go to playgrounds because many children had accidents there, myself included.

On one occasion, in 1973, a few school friends and I passed by the playground opposite Naledi ya Meso, the crèche I went to with Levi until 1970. Seeing that there were no bullies around, we took advantage of the situation. This being second nature to us boys, we had to challenge one another. On this occasion, as we had done on several occasions before, it was on the steel horse which bounced back and forth. The challenge was to see who could ride the horse until it reached maximum height. At that point, it was known that the horse was at its most dangerous, hence the challenge to reach the highest point. We all took our turns until it was mine. I rode the horse and felt on top of the world every time it came close to maximum height. The indicator of maximum height was its turning point, which was also at zero velocity. This meant that the horse actually stood still for a moment, and that was really the aim of the whole challenge, to reach zero velocity. On this occasion, as I reached maximum height the horse seemed to turn around and head downwards before my body was ready for it, leaving me suspended in mid air. My body met the robust steel horse as it spiralled up again and I was propelled into the air and fell to the ground with my weight on my left arm. It was extremely painful, but like most pains I had experienced while playing, I ignored it and thought it would be fine by the time I reached home. It was not to be.

At home I struggled for more than half an hour to remove my jersey. The problem was that I could not lift my left arm. Finally my aunt, who was visiting that day, came to check what was taking me so long. "Ausie!" she called out to my mother after she had helped me out of the jersey. "Come and see the miracle I am seeing here."

"What!" my mother came into the bedroom.

"I think the child is badly hurt."

"What happened?" my mother asked in a sharp, yet worried tone.

"The other big boys were chasing us with dogs on our way from school, and ... and ... I fell into a hole," I lied because of the stern warnings my mother had dished out on several occasions about not going to the playgrounds.

"Do you know where these boys live?" my mother asked. "Your father will have to do something about this."

"Eh ... I have never seen them before," I continued the lie.

"I think he has broken his arm," my aunt now interposed with urgency after inspecting my arm for the umpteenth time, thus saving me from any more lies.

I was rushed to Baragwanath Hospital. There I was examined by a doctor who explained to my mother and aunt that I had dislocated my elbow in the fall.

A thought came to mind: I wished they would confine me to a hospital bed. Not that I liked hospitals more than I would have liked to play with my friends. What appealed to me was the idea of being brought all the good food and sweets that were brought to people in hospital. I was thinking of all the fruit, drink, biscuits, cakes, and specially cooked Sunday food that I had seen taken to people in hospital. Besides, I would have gone through an experience none of my friends had been through. That would be a big plus for me. I could just imagine myself saying to my friends: "Have you ever slept in a hospital? I'm telling you, sonny, it's not child's play. I was there. Have you ever broken your arm? It's bloody painful, I know, I have been through that." But it was not to be, and in the end I had to settle for the dislocated elbow part of the story.

But to get back to Jimmy. What I liked most about Jimmy was not what he had. It was his sister, Sophia. To my boyhood eyes she was the most beautiful girl ever seen. Being at Jimmy's place afforded me the opportunity to be close to Sophia as well. Sophia was light in complexion and had a smooth skin with delicate lips and big clear brown eyes. Her body was neither fat nor thin, rather solid, but attractive. Looking at her legs in her black dungarees at school took my breath away. (For some reason, we called the black sleeveless school dresses dungarees.)

But of course I did not have the guts to even suggest to her that I wanted to be with her; after what had happened with Nokuthula, any hanky-panky was out of the question.

But speaking of Jimmy and money, money was so scarce we used to appreciate even one cent. I remember the time Thabang picked up one cent and the three of us, Thabang, Levi and I, rushed to the shops. We bought one ice mint candy, which was less than a square inch in size, and happily shared it among the three of us. What we did was to take the sweet while it was still in its wrapper and gently crush it with a stone. We then unwrapped the sweet and began the impossible task of sharing the pieces equally. In the end, it was the one who found the money who came away with the biggest share.

Things were done differently with a school friend of mine who I only remember as Chomi. For some unknown reason we ended up calling each other Chomi, which was slang for friend. If we had one sweet between us, he would unwrap the sweet, put it in his mouth, and break it with his teeth. This meant I had to eat a piece of sweet that came out of his mouth. I use to wipe the saliva-lined sweet against my – usually dirty – pants before I threw it into my mouth.

With another lower primary school friend, Banke, I had yet another method for sharing scarce resources. We managed to perfect an act which resulted in our gaining things for nothing. We picked certain shops, being very careful who our targets in those shops were going to be. Most of our stunts were carried out on women behind the counter.

What we did was to go into the shop when the shop was really busy. We would wait at the counter and target the busiest saleslady among the lot. After standing around for a while, we would pretend to another assistant that we had given the very busy assistant money and were still waiting for her to give us our sweets. Our story would be: "We gave her two cents and she hasn't given us our sweets." The targeted saleslady, hearing this, would come out fuming, "Voetsek, voetsek. You are mad. You did not give me any money!" Banke would start crying. He had flexible tear ducts which never failed him. At the flick of an eyelid he could produce torrents of tears that fell down his cheeks. I would attempt to join him. Now, with his round dark face in tears and my innocent-looking face on the verge of tears, the woman behind the counter would often end up giving in to our demands. As we walked out of the shop with our two cents worth of sweets, Banke would wipe the tears from his face and threaten the saleslady that next time he was going to tell his father. I don't know how he ever talked me into that one, but I always went along with it. In most cases it worked. When Banke's parents moved him from Ikaneng Lower Primary School to another school the act ended, as I did not have the nerve to carry out the scheme alone.

My main chores around the house were to clean the silverware, the water storage bucket, the paraffin Primus stove, and scrub the toilet. They were not difficult tasks, it's just that they were time-consuming – especially shining the countless little pieces of silverware my mother had out on the display cabinet. Negotiating the crevices and contours of the myriad pieces of complicated silverware with a cloth and a dab of white Silvo was no easy task. Often I had to use a matchstick to remove the Silvo paste that collected in the little grooves. This seemed to take forever, especially when my whole being was dedicated to doing one thing and one thing only – playing.

There was one other big job that I had, which kept me from playing: I had to make the fire for cooking in our Ellis coal stove. Those who grew up with electricity do not know what they missed. The process of making fire in a coal stove was a major operation. There were several different techniques used in making a coal stove fire that required a good knowledge of procedure, trouble-shooting, short-cuts, and a good eye for the dangers involved. Imagine me at age nine, with an axe bigger than myself, having to chop wooden blocks for the fire, then having to poke the old ash out of the stove, then placing tightly rolled newspaper into the bottom of the fire chamber, then arranging the chopped wood on top of that, and finally setting the fire alight with a little match. In addition to that, once the wood started to burn, you had to pour pieces of coal slowly and skilfully on top of the burning wood, making sure that you encouraged rather than suffocated the fire. When that was done, you had to dash outside and watch the chimney for smoke. If no smoke was to be seen, the smoke was inside the house rather than where it should be, coming out of the chimney, and you knew that it was time to climb onto the roof by standing on one of the window handles – another risky manoeuvre. Once, I remember, the window handle made a hundred-and-eighty-degree turn, leaving me face down, caressing the ground. Once you were on the roof, you had to take a long pole with a ball of cloth attached to one end and start clearing the chimney. By that time, the chances of your fire developing into the sort of furnace needed for cooking were next to zero. The best thing was to start the fire again from scratch.

But for boys like us, who did not have time for anything except play, that was out of the question. Restarting the fire meant you had to reverse the process. This meant picking out the unburnt pieces of coal from the fire chamber, one by one, and placing them back into the coal bucket. You then had to remove any remnants of wood, in most cases still burning hot, and then start the whole process all over again. There was, however, a short-cut, but a very dangerous one. All you had to do was reach for the paraffin, pour it on top of the old fire materials, and re-ignite the fire without all the hassles of having to start over again.

Someone once gave me a tip about a product faster than paraffin – methylated spirits. I tried it once and thought I saw a ghost that day. Because of playing with my friends, I was late home to make the fire. You see, you had to make the fire at the right time. Being early meant that the fire would already be too weak when my sisters returned from school and needed to start cooking. On the other hand, if the fire was made late, I would have to explain to my parents why the fire wasn't ready on time. That particular day, as usually happens with things you are in a hurry to do, the fire did not want to burn as it should. On the advice I had been given, I took the bottle of methylated spirits and poured some of it onto the fire. As I lifted the bottle after pouring, the flame followed me and was creeping across my arm at the speed of a snake. In fright, I let go of the bottle. The bottle fell to the ground and the burning spread all over the kitchen, transforming the floor into a pool of blue and orange flames. You should have seen how I dashed for the water bucket in the kitchen and poured it all over the kitchen floor. Then I rushed to the water tap outside and filled the bucket once more and threw it over the kitchen floor again.

I thought it was a miracle that I had subdued the flames, but I ended up having to get down on my hands and knees to scrub both the kitchen and dining room floors, then wax them to make sure they were left with a sparkle. That day I had even less time left for playing.

The fact that resources were scarce, especially in the toy department, did not discourage us from playing and having fun. It was only the Jimmys of Soweto who could afford toys, and this was maybe one in a thousand children. Making the best of a bad situation, we ended up playing with some strange toys and making up some strange games as well.

The simplest toy was a brick, representing a motor vehicle, a bus in particular. Best of all, one could get bricks almost anywhere. Another inventive toy was the self-made phone. The phone, however, was only possible to make if you stumbled upon a broken portable radio. We would dismantle the radio, the way we knew best – by stoning it until it fell to pieces. We would then salvage the transformer and unwind the copper wire. To each end of the unwound wire we would attach the blue inside container of a match box. The result, as long as we did not touch any part of the wire which interfered with the transmission, was a two-way "telephone" on which we had hours of fun, ending only when the fragile copper wire eventually snapped.

In summer, we hunted for locusts in the open veld adjacent to the school. We would take the locusts and thread them, with a little cotton, to the blue inside container of a match box. We would then emulate the great chariot race from Ben Hur, with locusts as our horses and match box containers as our carts.

Yet another game, and probably the hardest of them all, was

bird hunting. As well-practised as some of us were at stone-throwing, stoning birds was a futile exercise and so we made ketis – hand catapults. I must admit that I was good at making ketis, but was never good enough at shooting them to kill a bird or any of the other prey that we hunted, which included rats. There was a certain kind of rat which was lauded for its palatability. It was called a strepi because of the light stripes on its back. Hunting rats was no easy task, especially in the middle of the day. I still remember how I used to envy the gang of boys who lived next to the shops. Often, on their way back from rat hunting at the mine dumps, they would pass us by with a row of skinned rats spread-eagled along a steel wire.

My friends and I tried several times to catch strepis, but without success. It was not only its legendary cherished taste that made me want to eat a rat that badly, there was another reason.

It was said that eating a rat could cure the problem of boys wetting their beds at night – one of my big problems. Curing that problem would release the incredible hold my sisters had over me. They always threatened, "We will tell your friends that you wet your blankets last night." If my friends ever heard that secret I was doomed. How could I walk boldly next to them once I had the reputation of a "bed-wetter"? I would be the laughing stock of the entire block and beyond. Such revelations had a tendency of travelling all the way to school. And what about Sophia?

Always when I wet my bed I found I was also urinating in a dream ... except for one occasion I will never forget. I woke up screaming, shouting that there were people trying to steal Gilbert, my physically disabled brother. "Ntate, ba utswa Gilbert. Ba tswa le ene ka lefensetere!" – Daddy, they are stealing Gilbert and they are taking him with them through the window! I screamed like a wild person from my mattress in the dining room. I was so scared I was shivering, and as I discovered, I was also weeing in my bed. It took my mother more than an hour to calm me down. I was so ashamed I did not know how I was going to survive the humiliation of having my mother wash and hang up my sleeping gear because of the terrible mess I had caused. From that night on my parents made me sleep on the floor in their bedroom. From that night on, too, I decided I would call for my mother immediately I realised I was wetting my bed so that she could light the candle for me and I could use seruwa – chamber pot. The problem with seruwa was that I had to wake up before any of my brothers or sisters, to dispose of its contents down the toilet. No self-respecting boy my age wanted to be seen carrying seruwa around.

My desperate attempts to catch a rat never succeeded. But I ended up solving the problem of my bed-wetting all by myself, and in another way. What I did was to ask myself every time I went to urinate: "Am I not dreaming?". Somehow, after only a couple more "accidents", this method solved my problem permanently.

But back to games. The very best game was target practice with stones. This was more than just a game, it was a pragmatic requirement for survival. What we did was to arrange empty canned food tins on top of each other. Then, just as we did when practising on school windows, we would decide how far from the target we were going to stand. What followed was a very serious process of keeping score of who hit the tins most. Being good at target practice also developed one's reputation on the street. There were boys with the reputation of stoning stray dogs to death with a single stone. Even half of such a reputation served as a deterrent to bullies and was useful in gaining respect among one's equals.

Thieves, thugs and rascals

Reputation was very important across the township. And we revered especially those who were notorious. In the early seventies, like most children of the townships, we did not know much about the "good guys", those who were doing something to improve our status as blacks. Instead, most of our role models came from the streets and our larger-than-life silver screen idols.

I think what attracted us to the "bad guys" was the fact that they were feared around the township and were always running away from the police, just as we were in our games. From first-hand experience, every time we saw policemen around we knew someone was going to be arrested, and in most cases the arrest was brutal. Naturally enough, our view of policemen was that of ugly and fearsome people, especially the big-chested white ones from Brixton Murder and Robbery Squad. "I will go and call Brixton for you!" was the threat always made by parents whenever their older teenage sons were being disobedient or running into trouble.

The savageness with which the Brixton Murder and Robbery Squad used to handle suspects was legendary. So every time we saw thugs and hooligans being chased by the police, we actually felt pity for them, and this also gave rise to a certain deeply etched solidarity with them. Rather than seeing them for what they were, we youngsters idolised them as the brave victims of police ferociousness.

In emulation of the township gangs, we started making our own handmade wooden knives, and in mock fights we would pretend to be them, calling our group the Bra So-and-so's, depending on which gang was in favour at the particular time. The reality for the victims of the gangs we mimicked with such ease and boisterousness, was that the knife was a dangerous weapon and many people died unnecessarily by its blade. The best known knife of the era was the okapi knife, or ghoni, as it was known in the township at the time.

There were thieves, thugs and gangsters who were feared for their mastery of the knife. Watching them in a knife fight was spectacular. Usually, their aim was not to deliver a fatal blow but rather a series of light wounds that would teach their challenger a lesson and have him running for his life. It was well known that a knife in the hands of a farm-boy turned street-fighter was the most deadly weapon. The theory went that because of their lack of experience in street fighting, instead of merely scratching their opponents on the surface of the skin, they would drive the knife all the way in, resulting in death.

There was a man known as Boy-Boy who lived in Zone Three. He was one of those notorious for having stabbed more people to death than any knife-wielding thug across our area. Some of the boys at school, like Lewis, who lived in the same street as Boy-Boy, told us that the police could not catch him. He had it on good word from his older brother that Boy-Boy had said he could "feel" the police from a distance. Some people said that he was helped in his exploits by his granny who masterminded the "magic of the nights".

On the other hand there was Joey. Joey was notorious for his left-hand clap. I do not know how true it was, but I heard that he once clapped a girl so hard the poor thing fell into a coma and never recovered. Joey was a young man with a tiny body, but his clap gave him a reputation unequalled by any at the time. I remember the day I came face to face with Joey. I was sent to the shops with a five-rand note. As I was going through the last passage before I reached the shops, Joey appeared from nowhere. I froze as he came straight towards me. "Hey, sonny, come here," he ordered me. "What do you have in your hand?"

"Nothing," I forced the words from my mouth, trying to conceal my fear.

"Open your hand," he said grabbing me by my trouser leg, and shouted as I tried to resist, "I'll clap you!" The mere mention of the word clap released my grip on the five-rand note and Joey took it.

Usually when something like that happened, as I retreated I would look for stones and start throwing them. But not this time – not with the likes of Joey around. The worst part was that he was among those who lingered around the shops where I was sent almost every day.

On reaching home I told my family that a huge man who I had never seen before, carrying a knife as long as my arm, robbed me of the money. My brother, Moropa, was furious. It had been his money. He jumped up, grabbed one of his golf sticks, and said, "Let's go, I want you to show me this big guy!" I was surprised by his reaction. I had never seen any of my brothers in a fight with anyone before. But the way he looked and acted I felt confident that if we caught the culprit my brother was going to show him a thing or two. I was already imagining the sort of protected aura I would possess if we found Joey and my brother bliksemed – beat the devil out of – him. Such news would travel to school and I would be elevated in everyone's eyes. My brother and I headed for the shops but we never found any sign of Joey.

Then there was the leader of the Madamara gang, Mandla–Sandlana – sandlana meaning one-handed. To be a gang leader with one hand was something outstanding, something so outstanding as to be revered. I remember the day the Madamaras fought a gang called Top Seven in the street adjacent to my house. The leader of the Top Seven was a man called Seuntjie, a tall pitch-black fellow with snow-white teeth and red eyes. On that day the lids of the metal rubbish bins which normally stood next to people's front gates were all lifted by gang members for use as shields. Some gang members brandished knives while others were armed with tomahawks. The blades of pangas also blazed in the air.

The young boys, like ourselves, who wanted to see their idols in action and wanted especially to be able to relay the story to those who were not around, stood just inside the safety of their front gates. Before the battle began Mandla-Sandlana called out to one such boy to be his assistant. This boy, Oscar, was to supply Mandla-Sandlana with stones or bricks until the two gangs were close enough for hand-to-hand combat. All of a sudden I was more interested in Oscar than I was in Mandla-Sandlana.

As the battle raged Oscar was to be seen running in rhythm with Mandla-Sandlana. He was right there in the battle zone making sure Mandla-Sandlana was armed with a continuous supply of ammunition. In Oscar's little hands he could only carry two half bricks at a time. This meant that almost as soon as he had handed Mandla-Sandlana the bricks, he had to dash off again to find two more bricks to be back before Mandla-Sandlana's supply was depleted. Oscar also had to make sure that he was not in anybody's way. As if that was not enough, he also had to avoid flying stones, some of them as big as his small head.

After the battle, I came out from behind the tree which was behind our front fence, from where I had watched the whole bloody scene. All the other young boys also emerged from behind their front fences. We all gathered around Oscar – the man of the moment. Mandla-Sandlana had even rewarded Oscar's bravery with a two-cent piece.

We stood in awe of Oscar. The likes of Mandla-Sandlana were known for taking money from boys not giving it to them. What Oscar did that day was the envy of every boy, those who were there and those to whom the story would soon be related. To think that I was hiding behind my fence behind a dense, tall tree while he was part of the battle ... Little Oscar was on his way straight into the local gangster chronicles. He was an instant legend.

Elijah – not the boy who was in my class but dropped out of school, another Elijah – was a renowned rascal around town. The story of my boyhood would be incomplete without including Elijah. Elijah lived just a street away from me, and was renowned for stealing cars. It took me a while to realise that Elijah was nothing but a thief, and although he was also known to wield a knife, at least he was not known to be a bully like Joey or Boy-Boy or most of the others. His sole interest was stealing. But what made Elijah's car stealing operation interesting – if not incredulous – was the fact that he was always caught. What I, and many others, could never figure out was why he always had to take the stolen car to his home to wash it. He seemed to have an obsession with washing stolen cars. His modus operandi was always the same – steal a car and take it home to wash. The police must have long ago figured that out, because he was always caught while washing his stolen car.

One day he really went overboard. He stole a herd of cattle. No one had ever driven a herd of cattle into the township ... one cow, one bull, yes, but not a herd. He drove the herd all the way into his yard. That was how he operated, he would steal whatever he wanted and take it home, the first place the police would come and look for it.

That day meat was cheap. One rand bought a heaped plateful of beef. People were going up and down the street with plates and bowls full of meat. "I'd rather starve than buy stolen meat," was my mother's response when the other women told her about the meat bargain. "Anyway, I am not mad about beef. My father used to own herds of cattle when I was a little girl back in Thabazimbi."

The going up and down with dishes of meat reminded me of the day a horse was hit by a coal truck on the corner of our street. I had heard that the Basotho ate horsemeat but dismissed it as nonsense. That day, within seconds of the horse falling to the ground, I saw men and women shooting out from nowhere onto the scene. They had all sorts of cutting paraphernalia in their hands; women stood there with big dishes in their hands while the men busied themselves dismembering the horse without even skinning it. I felt my stomach turn. "Ntja-mme," "E-kgolo," "Moholowane," "A ko o butle," "E re ke engathe weso," Sesotho exclamations were flying around with the same rapidity as the action of those involved.

This time the meat was coming not from a dead horse but from Elijah and his stolen cattle. The next morning Jub-Jub, Elijah's little brother, whose nickname was the result of sucking his thumb continuously even at the age of ten, was seen roaming the streets with a piece of roasted steak in his hand. You could still see the sleep heavily on his eyes and that he had not even washed yet. But it was a feast for everyone. That same afternoon Elijah was picked up by the police and the remaining cows were taken away.

There was another day involving Elijah I will never forget. It was the day Levi's oldest sister stood up against Elijah. I mean she, Gwyn, stood there in the middle of the road armed with nothing but confidence and an acidic tongue, lashing out at Elijah left and right. "A'never o nchape. A'never!" She warned Elijah that he would never dare beat her up, never – come to think of it, that word a'never was a typical township creation that grew to include all the personal references to the word never, for example, it could be used to mean, he'll never, she'll never, you'll never, I'll never. Knowing that Elijah wielded a knife, I feared for Gwyn's life. But she stood her ground shouting that Elijah should take a good look at her and that he would never dare touch her. Elijah had obviously pressed a wrong button – although popular, this wrong button phrase always confused me. I knew of buttons on the radio and on shirts but not for a minute, at that age, could I imagine where buttons could be located on a person's body. Levi was now standing at his sister's side, a stone in his hand concealed behind his tiny back; though I don't think his presence, or his stone, would have made an iota of difference to Elijah. "Why don't you try it." Gwyn went on and on and I felt like telling her, for her own safety, to shut up and run back into the house, especially at that moment when Elijah started to stomp aggressively towards her. "You just touch me and I will show you a ghost," she shouted into his approaching face. I was relieved when Elijah pulled back and went home. To this day I ask myself, what would have happened if Elijah had produced a knife and decided on a different course of action? But what amazes me even more is that, single-handedly, Gwyn managed to stare Elijah down. Elijah must have pressed one hell of a wrong button. But Gwyn deserved a ten for bravery.

Two streets away, towards the mine dumps, there lived a man I knew as Terror. He was a man who died many times and yet, surprisingly enough, was still alive. I never knew another person who was pronounced dead on so many occasions. The first time I saw him after he had been pronounced dead, was on a Saturday morning. The night before, the news was all over the streets that Terror had been stabbed to death and his body found covered in blankets next to the Zone Four shops. Yet the next day, there he was, alive and well, walking around the streets. The first time I was surprised, but as this performance was repeated several times, I eventually started to disbelieve anyone who claimed to have seen Terror's dead body.

Talking of dead bodies, they became such a common sight that other boys would actually tease you if you told them that you had never seen a real dead body on the streets before. There was a time when we bragged about how many dead bodies we had seen. And you did not just claim that you had seen a dead body. You had to explain whose body it was, exactly when you saw it, where you saw it, who saw you seeing the body ... and to show you were really connected on ma-bare-bare – the grape vine – you should also have a good idea of who actually carried out the killing.

I used to think that the people who went around inflicting pain on others were immune to pain. Gratefully, I soon found out I was wrong. I remember the day Siphiwe, another knife-wielding thug, was stabbed in the chest right below the clavicle. Siphiwe was Mirabela's older brother. "Please someone, take me to hospital," he cried out as he clasped his white T-shirt against the bleeding wound.

"I don't want to die, please." I actually felt happy that he was going through so much pain, and not because I was a little sadist. The feeling was generated by an incident which had taken place a few weeks before. Gilbert, my brother, was watering the lawn. Siphiwe was passing by and Gilbert accidentally splashed a few drops of water on him. I remember Siphiwe's exact words: "You are watering me, you fokon cripple." I was enraged that day. How could he talk to my brother like that! If there was anything I could have done that day, I would have done it, I was so hurt by what he said. So when I saw him there, in pain, I just stood by and savoured the moment, happy to learn that those who inflicted pain could also feel pain ... bloody rascal.

The same applied to the rascal Geelboy, who had robbed me of my flute-sweet three years back. He was captured by the Jaws gang from Zone One. The slogan for this gang, which took its name from the Jaws movie, was "Ya mo gabola jaws", meaning "Jaws tears him apart". The gang dragged Geelboy to his home, and in front of his mother, his shoes were taken off. He was then slashed with a knife under his feet. His mother screamed madly at the violators of her son. But Geelboy only bellowed at her, "Shut up, mamma. Shut up!" because the more she screamed the more the gang stabbed him. I, a little boy standing across the road from his house, wished the gang would carry on slashing those feet until he could walk no more. It was a good lesson to the nasty thief of my coveted flute-sweet.

Passing away

Early in 1975 my father passed away at home after a long struggle with illness. That morning, before he died, my eldest brother and I were sent to fetch my grandmother on my father's side who lived in Garankuwa, north of Pretoria. The generous Ntate Molatlhegi, a truck driver who lived three streets away from us, provided us with the transport, as he had done throughout my father's illness. Ntate Molatlhegi was always available when my family needed him to take my father to the doctor or anywhere else that my father needed to go in search of better health.

That afternoon when we returned home from Garankuwa, my sister, Lesego, called me aside. "I hope you won't cry," she said. "Father has passed away." I was silent for a while. I was trying to figure out why she was expecting me to cry. I did not see any reason why I was supposed to cry. Even if I had to cry, I thought, it would not be in the presence of my older brothers or sisters. What would people say if they saw me, a boy, crying, and especially in the presence of girls?

"How could you hide this from me?" I heard my grandmother, who was really old at that time, shouting from the bedroom. "Why didn't you tell me straight away the reason why I was being brought here?" She sounded pretty upset.

Many people from the township came to the house to give their condolences to my family. But, as for me, I remained pretty much unaffected by what had happened. I think the reason was that over the past three years I had seen less and less of my father. Most of the time he was in hospital or away in Pretoria or other places for treatment. My mother even left her job of washing and ironing in Johannesburg's northern suburbs so that she could take care of my father. During that period, Moropa and Kgofa, who were busy with their Junior Certificate – Form Three or Grade Ten – were forced to leave high school and had to get jobs so that they could help my oldest brother who was the only one in the family working at the time.

And I must say my brothers worked as a team. I remember every Friday afternoon they would arrive home with a big paper bag full of groceries. The financial gap that was left when both my mother and father stopped earning, was covered well. One day, as Levi and I licked our fingers through the crumbs of a 12.5 kg empty sugar bag, Levi exclaimed: "I wish I lived here. You always eat nice food. Your brothers always bring you lots of sweets on a Friday."

After about a week of mourning, and visitors coming in and out of the house, Saturday came and I was told that I had to go and see my father for the last time in his coffin. There was a queue of people winding its way into the bedroom where his body lay. Observing men emerging from the room with twisted faces and women who were weeping openly, I became more and more interested in what it was that they were seeing that could be so terrible. At that stage in my life I had seen scores of horror movies and I wondered if what I would see would frighten me.

Finally it was my turn, and I walked slowly into the bedroom. I saw my father lying inside a big wooden coffin. But I did not see anything terrifying. My mother, standing beside me, told me this was the last time I would be seeing my father and asked me to say, "Robala ka kgotso ntate," which meant simply "Rest in peace, father." I did this and left the room more or less unmoved and wondering what the twisted and tearful faces were all about.

Later that morning, while sombre hymns were sung, the men lifted the coffin into a bakkie which was waiting outside our house. My mother and I, as well as close relatives and some of my mother's confidantes, climbed into the back of the bakkie and sat around the coffin. We were heading for the St James Anglican Church in Zone Three, next to the Zone Three shops. As the bakkie and other cars, as well as people on foot, made their way slowly to the church, I saw children squat, kneel, and sit flat on the pavement as the funeral procession passed. I saw older men taking off their hats and bowing their heads and folding their arms. This was a sign of respect which was observed by all irrespective of the stature of the deceased. Even for hardened criminals who terrorised the community, the sign of respect was the same. I did not know why we did it, but it was done by all without any questions asked. I recall the day Jimmy decided not to squat or sit when a funeral procession passed by. A young man we knew to be nothing more than a hooligan threatened to kick Jimmy's backside if he did not show his respects like everyone else. This form of respect for funerals was unchallengeable.

For a while I sat there in the bakkie, my eyes glued to the coffin. I was not aware of what was happening when I felt my mother's handkerchief wiping away the tears that were rolling down my cheeks. For the first time since the news of my father's death, I was crying.

At the graveyard, when they lowered the coffin into the ground, I felt a lump rising in my throat as it dawned on me that I would never see my father again. I tried to stop the tears, but there seemed nothing I could do to hold back the drizzle. Mucus started clogging my nostrils and before I knew it I was crying again.

I remembered the day when I was in Sub B and my father took me Christmas shopping. Normally us children went with my mother to buy new clothes which we wore on New Year's day. That year my father insisted that he was taking me alone. "I want this boy to choose the kind of clothes he wants. Every time you," he said, referring to my mother and sisters, "take him shopping you buy him majaja" – the opposite to good clothes.

Standing at his side, and reaching just above his knee, I felt very proud as we boarded a bus into town. It was one of the most memorable days of my childhood walking side by side with my father in downtown Johannesburg. He took me to Minty's, the Indian clothing store, where he normally did his shopping.

"Now you must look carefully and choose the kind of clothes you want," my father said to me as he walked up to the light-skinned man who was standing behind the counter. He spoke to the man in what appeared to be English.

I was nervous at the sight and the presence of this man who looked to me like a white man. I ended up picking a green cotton suit, a light green shirt, a green tie to match the suit, and a green hat with a yellow feather on the side.

"Are you sure this is what you want?" I just nodded, watching the white-looking man out of the corner of my eyes. "Now get yourself some shoes," my father said.

The first shoes I laid my eyes on were brown school shoes. I picked them out without any further waste of time. I put them on, and my father asked, "Do they fit you okay?" Again I nodded. This time the white-looking man was standing very near to us. The truth was that the shoes were tight. I was afraid that if I said no before this man, I might get roughed up just like I had seen white policemen rough up people in the township.

When we reached home and I showed my brothers what I had bought, they laughed at my choice of green, but I did not care because I had picked all the clothes by myself.

I also remembered how my father used to send me to place bets for him at the house where they played the Chinese gambling game township folk referred to as fahfi. Every time my father won, he would send me to buy baked beans, eggs and bread. That combination of food was not standard fare in our household and was normally eaten only when my father had won, which made it special food.

The tears streamed from my eyes as I stared down into my father's grave, but those recollections helped to ease the pain.

School outings

My first school outing was a trip to the Pretoria Zoo. I was in Sub A, in 1971.

The night before the trip I did not sleep. I dreamt the bus left without me. That morning I got out of bed earlier than normal and the first thing I did was check whether all my provisions were in place. I had a tomato and egg sandwich, some fruit, a small packet of Simba Chips and a "groovy" of Fanta. You may well ask what kind of drink this was. You see, when soft drinks in cans first hit the shops in the township, they came in the form of a brand known as Groovy. Since then, it became popular for canned soft drink to be referred to as a "groovy", hence a "groovy of Fanta". As a small boy, we grew up calling toothpaste "colgate", a plastic bag was "checkers", chips were "simba", and powdered soap was "surf". Well-known brand names were immortalised for us in common nouns. To this day I still think of many of these products in terms of those names.

As far as the trip to the zoo went, there was nothing outstanding to me about seeing animals; the real excitement lay in getting out of school and going somewhere in a big bus. After all, I was never an animal lover – not with the tough time dogs gave me. As a result, rather than the zoo, my main memory of the trip was the accident we saw on our way back.

A young white woman's Volkswagen beetle was involved in an accident and when we passed by, we saw her lying on the side of the road with blood on her legs. I remember relating the story a few weeks later to my aunt who worked as a domestic in the Johannesburg suburb of Killarney. "This white sister's leg was broken," I explained excitedly.

But my aunt laughed out loud. "It's not a white sister," she said trying to catch her breath, "she is called 'missies'." From what I had been taught, any female who was older than me but much younger than my mother, was my sister. No one had explained to me that the person had to be black to qualify for the title. I did not know it was wrong to call the white woman at the side of the road sister – until the day my aunt taught me otherwise.

The other thing I remember from that first school outing, was how I enjoyed the singing in the bus as we returned home. We all raised our voices loudly and proudly and sang songs we had been taught at school.

My sisters and many other kids' brothers and sisters were at the school waiting for the bus to return. But my sisters were not interested in how the trip had been. Their first question was: "Where is makgaritla?" – left-overs? I handed them my small school bag and they went through it and found some fruit, which seemed to make them very happy.

From that trip until 1975 I went on all the school excursions. That is, until late 1975 when an incident saw me stop going on any school trips at all.

The school had arranged an outing to go and see the stage play Umabatha at Jabulani Amphitheatre. At that time three of my brothers were working as well as my mother, who had gone back to work after my father's death. Everybody was talking about Umabatha around the township and I came home from school that afternoon all excited about going to see the play. There was no doubt in my mind that I was going to see the play because my family never refused me any money to go on a school outing.

But when it came to Umabatha it seemed things had suddenly changed. "There is no money for that," my mother replied when I asked her for the fifty cents for the play. I could not believe my ears. There were four people earning a wage in our household and they were saying they were unable to raise fifty cents.

At the time my oldest brother, Motsietsi, worked for a tinned food company. I remember him telling us that they supplied tinned bully beef to the army. At first I just could not imagine soldiers eating in war. To my mind, soldiers did nothing but shoot each other. "From what I have heard," Motsietsi once explained, "every day each soldier gets a few cans of different kinds of tinned food." Again, I could not believe my ears. Not only soldiers eating but one man getting more than one can of tinned food, while we shared one tin of food among the whole family. Instantly, joining the army became an attractive possibility to me.

As for Kgofa, he worked for a company which sold eggs. At first I thought they *made* eggs there until someone reminded me that eggs were laid by chickens. What I remember about Kgofa's job was that he and his friends always brought home big boxes of eggs. They said they had skoti – from the Zulu word umgodi, meaning a hole – at work. Now that stretched my imagination. I thought work was a nice place to be, based on my brothers' stories and what they earned and brought home, and now they were talking about a hole at work. To make matters even more mysterious and wonderful, the hole was associated with boxes of eggs. I tried to imagine a box containing something like sixty trays of eggs and near it a hole, but I could come up with nothing concrete. In the end I abandoned the quest for logic and simply appreciated the fact that skoti brought us lots of eggs. As for Moropa, I was not interested in where he worked, because their product was not related to food.

For the whole week before the trip to Umabatha, I begged for the money and the answer was the same over and over again. Depressed, I thought about what happened at school on the days that children went on an outing. It only brought on more misery: in most cases, those who did not go on the outing were bundled into one class and told to shut up and read their books, as if it were their fault or a sin that they were not going.

Some of these children's parents struggled to pay their school fees, let alone lunches and trips and school uniforms. There was one boy we called Chippa – after Chippa Moloi of Orlando Pirates – because of his prowess on the soccer field. His parents couldn't even afford to buy him a school tie, and he was always being punished for it at lower primary school. Chippa ended up stringing a piece of dirty cloth he picked up from the school dumping area around his neck so that he could avoid being punished for coming to school without a tie.

I always felt pity for the students who never went on a single outing. They looked like outcasts with sad little faces. Now it was my turn to join the outcasts. My heart was bleeding. At home they always did their best to ensure that whatever was needed for school was provided. But on this occasion, the answer remained an emphatic no.

Strangely, on the day of the outing, sitting in the silent classroom with the forlorn outcasts, I felt at one with them. I was identifying with them and I liked the feeling. That day I made a decision that from then on I was not going to bother my family about money for trips or outings any longer. And from then on the only exceptions I ever made were outings to school athletics and music competitions, which were compulsory. It took my mother and brothers more than five years before they finally realised that I had boycotted all school outings.

"Aren't you going to Durban?" my mother asked one evening when we were eating supper. "I was with Mma Maropeng and she was buying provisions and a big bag for luggage for her daughter. She goes to the same school as you, doesn't she?"

"Yes," I replied without interest. "Her name is Popie."

"When is the trip to Durban?" Moropa asked.

"Tomorrow," I said.

"Tomorrow?" Kgofa exclaimed in amazement.

"But why didn't you tell us?" Abuti Motsietsi joined in.

"I did not think there would be money for it," I replied, "just like there was no money for Umabatha when I was in primary school."

"That was then," my mother said with concern. "Things are different now."

"Well, I am not interested anymore."

And that, for me, was the way it remained. Every time a trip or outing was announced, the memories of the Umabatha incident came rushing back to my mind and for the rest of my school life I never went on a school trip again.

Hostilities and altercations

My mother always warned me about playing in the mine dump areas, which were a stone's throw away from our house. To be honest, I also did not like going to the dumps as there were a couple of major dangers in the area. The first, and biggest, was the quicksand. In 1973, we buried a boy from our school who drowned in the quicksand as his friends ran back home crying for help. By the time his parents and other folk arrived to help, he was nowhere to be seen. I do not know how they ever dug him out of that mud.

Another boy, Lungi, found playing in the quicksand fun. He would submerge himself in the quicksand and breathe with the help of reeds. He dared anyone brave enough to do the same. My skin crawled whenever I saw him.

One day I decided that I was going to join my friends – there were about six of us – on an adventure to the mine dumps. On any expedition to the mine dumps it was advisable to go in a group – that way you were in a better position should you be attacked by other boys – the other great danger of venturing into the area.

We were going to the mine dumps to play spara-para. Spara-para was the art of running, zigzag, down the mine dumps without falling. Running down a mine dump was a bit like running down the grandstands at Orlando Stadium, only without the help of stairs

We played spara-para — running, zigzag, to the bottom — at these mine dumps, not heeding warnings to stay away.

and on loose sand. A part of the challenge was to see who could perform the most spectacular spara-para and reach the bottom in record time. I knew that my mother would not find out about my playing at the mine dumps because she was away at work and we were on school holidays. By the time she came home I would long be washed and shining with Vaseline.

When we reached the top of one of the mine dumps and were busy fooling around in preparation for our spara-para antics, some boys at the bottom of the dump called out to us.

"Come and play ball with us," they screamed.

"Where is the ball?" Levi screamed back.

We were immediately suspicious because we had never seen this group of boys before.

"Come down first and you will see it," one of them replied.

"Maybe this is a trap," I said to my younger friends. "I think we should get out of this place."

"Don't be a coward," Thabang laughed at me. But knowing Thabang as I did, it was easy to talk; he was the Ben Johnson of the group. When the going got tough, he normally outran all of us. I, on the other hand, was not much of a runner because of my breathing problems. At school the athletics teacher gave up on me because I could not run for long periods of time, and even the cruel methods which some of our teachers applied to bring out the athlete in a student, failed on me. What they used to do was to run after the stragglers with a whip, lashing out at the last one in the group. The method did nothing to make my breathing problems disappear, although it certainly did earn me a good few beatings. In the end I was forced to go to the clinic in Zone Three for a doctor's certificate to explain my condition.

Of course I would have loved to run as fast as, if not faster than, anyone else. I recall one year during the annual school athletics day at higher primary school, there was this boy, Harold, who became famous. I knew Harold because we lived in the same area and we used to walk to school together. Before that year's athletics meeting most students at the school did not even know Harold's name. But after his performance on the track, which stunned almost everyone, with firsts in the 100 metres, 200 metres, and 400 metres, and a second in the mile, everyone suddenly knew who Harold was. The next morning he was called out in front of the school assembly. I remember his smile and the confidence oozing from him as he stood up there with hands in his pockets. He was the hero of the school. I mean, who wouldn't want that?

Now, as we exchanged words with the boys at the bottom of the mine dump, the language turned vulgar. We felt no fear because there were no older people around. But then, as we climbed slightly down from our position, two older boys appeared with golf sticks in their hands.

"Who are you swearing at?" one of them asked with a serious look on his face.

"Didn't they teach you boys at home never to use vulgar language?" the second one added, swinging his stick around. The stern, older brother look on his face said it all, and I knew we were in trouble.

We started looking around for an escape route and one of the two older boys cautioned us.

"Don't even try it! You're coming down with us there to the boys you were swearing at."

I was not that worried about facing the boys down there, just as long as it was not these two older boys as well. On the whole, I had faith in my younger friends and knew that we could take good care of ourselves, as we had done several times before. When I think back to that moment – there were six of us and only two of them – I realise we could easily have scattered in all directions and in that way confused and outrun them. But somehow we obediently stood there and the two older boys led us away, herding us like cattle down to the bottom of the mine dump.

When we were finally at the bottom and facing our opposition, one of the older boys said, "Le lo shapa nkomane." I was not familiar with that phrase and it was not until they started pairing us off that I realised what shapa nkomane meant: "You will fight this one and you will fight that one; you with him and he with you." When it came to me, however, it was a case for debate. None of the kids from the opposition wanted to take me on because I was the oldest and the tallest in the mix.

"You wait one side," one of the older boys said. "Your turn will come."

I stood aside and watched my friends going one-on-one with their opponents. They didn't fare too badly, in fact most of them won their bouts. But when it came to my turn, one of the two older boys commanded, "Since you are the biggest, you will have to fight all of them at once." Without any further opportunity for debate, he gave the signal and they all charged at me at once, just like the quick, well-directed spittle from a gangster's mouth. I immediately retaliated, utilising all the karate moves I had learnt from the movies, and managed to keep them at bay. As the fighting continued I grabbed hold of one of the little boys and as he tried to break free, I tore his shirt from his back. That action saw the two older boys join in the fray with their golf sticks. Before I could say anything, fists, feet, sticks, stones, and whatever else could inflict pain, battered away at my body. In those moments my friends and I all saw the writing on the wall. There was only one thing to do: run for our dear lives, and we scattered in all directions.

Back at home that afternoon, while I was busy washing my beaten and bruised body, I wished I had listened to my mother's warning and never gone to play at the mine dumps.

A few months later, a boy called Ompie came to me asking for his tennis ball back. I had misplaced it and had looked for it everywhere and could not find it. Tennis balls were used by boys in the townships for several games except tennis. The older boys, and even sometimes adults, used tennis balls for a relaxing game called go teka. This game revolved around bouncing the ball from one person to the other with the use of one's feet. For the younger kids like us, tennis balls gave life to numerous games including eghie, bhati, marounders, di-beke, and soccer.

Ompie was a bit older than me and was an easy-going, likeable boy in my judgement. He was not like other older boys who would rough you up simply because they were older and stronger than you, claiming that because their status was like an older brother to you, they had the right to beat you. But when Ompie started pestering me about his tennis ball, I became irritated and ended up saying to him: "Am I supposed to shit the tennis ball because I can't find it?"

"Don't talk to me like that, sonny," he warned me that afternoon outside my house. "I asked you nicely."

"But I also told you that I can't find it," I raised my voice.

"What's wrong with you, sonny?" he approached closer. "Wa ngolozetsa – Are you grumbling at me – son?"

I did not reply but held my fists up in front of me and started thrashing the air with some of my boxing cum karate moves.

"My laetie. O nchovhela tsona – Are you shadow boxing for me, sonny? You want to fight me?" he said, looking at me in disbelief. But I just stood there and continued my warming up. I guess I must have had enough of being shunted around by older people and thought that I should embark on some sort of defiance campaign – starting with Ompie.

He came straight at me and unleashed a few blows, more like claps with his flat hands. Before I could even block one of them I found myself lying on the ground.

"You leave my little brother alone!" Lesego shouted from our gate.

"But he is the one who started all this," Ompie, who was younger than Lesego, explained.

"It does not matter whether he started it or not, leave him alone," Pontsho came up behind her. "Why don't you go and pick on someone your own age?"

"Don't you know that my brother has asthma?" Lesego now went on and on, and finally Ompie walked off, probably with the view that his tennis ball wasn't worth all the trouble.

After that debacle was over, I sat on the pavement outside our gate. I was grateful for my sisters' intervention, but there was something else. Their action brought on a whole lot of issues. There was the question of my reputation, which was now down the drain as far as my sisters were concerned. I was the one who was supposed to protect them from boys and not the other way round. Now they had something else to tease and blackmail me with if I tried anything nasty on them. On top of that, what would Ompie say about me to his friends and even some of my friends? Would he go around telling them that I was a weak, sick boy who could not take care of himself and had to be bailed out by his sisters?

I just sat there and shook my head. I could just imagine my sisters every time I made them angry: "You want us to call Ompie for you?" or "I'm not Ompie, you know, I will beat the hell out of you." This was not good at all.

When Levi, not long after this incident, approached me and said, "Let's go and take karate classes," I was more than willing.

I immediately asked, "Where?"

I was disappointed when he proposed S'amigo's. I was hoping he would say at the Moravian Hall in Zone Five, which was a long walk, but which was also where Tshepo, the boy who lived in the next street, went for classes. Those who had confronted Tshepo told us that he was stinking good at karate. I also played with him once and he threw a round-house kick to the back of my neck which stunned me.

Learning karate would give me the upper hand against the bullies, and others who were used to teasing me and beating me up. Apart from that, I was also attracted to the notion that karatekas were so disciplined that they never involved themselves in fights unless they were pushed to the absolute limit, and then, of course, they always taught the other person a good lesson. There was this man who I used to see jogging around in his gi – karate training uniform. They said he had been to Japan and could kill you with just one blow, but I had never seen him in a fight. To be surrounded by such an aura was something to die for. I could just imagine myself walking around with such a reputation under my belt ... bliksem!

The next day, Levi and I went off to S'amigo's dojo – karate gym – at the foot of the mine dumps, not far away from where my friends and I were involved in that fracas with the two older boys and all those smaller kids a few months back. The trainer's name, as with the dojo, was S'amigo. I later learnt that his name came from his continual use of the word amigo, picked up from Mexican cowboy movies which were so popular at the time. S'amigo's dojo was an open space among the reeds. There were eight long poles surrounding a rectangular area and on each of the poles candlesticks burnt to illuminate the dojo at night, especially necessary during the early sunset months of winter.

I enjoyed the training, but my brothers were disparaging.

"You, of all people, taking karate lessons?" mocked Moropa one weekend morning while we were drinking tea.

"You are wasting your time," added Kgofa. "You are too slow and too soft for a karateka."

"And who is your teacher?" asked Moropa.

"It's S'amigo," I answered.

"S'amigo!" Moropa shook his head.

"S'amigo is good," I defended. "He also trains in Japan," I exaggerated.

"Japan, my foot!" Moropa cut me down. "Is that what he told you? He is a bloody chance-taker, if you ask me." Moropa was not impressed at all by the Japan story. And he went on, "I think you should forget about this karate business and concentrate on other stuff. Because even if you could train for a hundred years, you will never be even as good as Bruce Lee's left finger."

I felt terribly hurt, but I continued to go with Levi to S'amigo's dojo for a few more weeks. With my brothers' words still jeering in the back of my head and in the face of S'amigo's cagey reputation, I eventually felt my heart drop out of it altogether. I would just continue to defend myself as best I could with the knowledge I gleaned from kung fu movies and the practical experience I gained from play-fighting.

Eating around

We were playing at my friend Jimmy's house one afternoon when his mother, a nursing sister at Beregwane or Parakwane – as the older folk used to call Baragwanath Hospital – brought us some cake. It was sliced and arranged beautifully on side plates. There were seven of us there, myself, Thabang, Levi, Mauwe, Mpho, Garry, and Jimmy of course.

"Come and get some cake, boys," Jimmy's mother called to us as we were tumbling all over the lawn. She was just as beautiful as her daughter, Sophia. All of us boys, with Jimmy leading the way, sprang up and walked towards her. I stood aside as each of my friends grabbed a piece.

"What about you?" she held a plate out towards me. "Don't you want some cake?"

In my heart I knew damn well that I wanted to eat that sumptuous-looking cake more than anything else. Cake some of us only ever got to eat over the Christmas period. And here was an opportunity to eat a whole piece of cake just like that. It was so painful for me to say to her, "No, I am not hungry." I felt like kicking myself.

"A well-taught boy," she praised me. "Not like the others," she looked towards my friends.

I sat there, watching in jealous silence, pretending that I was indeed fine and full, as the other boys licked at their cake. But what was occupying my mind was an incident a few weeks back at a wedding three streets away from where we lived. It was my mother's distant cousin's daughter's wedding. This cousin, Mma Moretlwa, as was custom, was normally called motswala, meaning cousin in Setswana. But we, my sisters and I, decided to extend her name to "Motswala-ha-ishe-o-fetse", meaning "Cousin, aren't you finished?" Every morning, at four a.m., when she arrived at our house to pick my mother up for work, she would knock on the door and call out, "Cousin, aren't you finished?" She and my mother, who were domestic workers in the northern suburbs of Johannesburg, would get the bus into town together. They were "staying out", meaning they did not live at their employers' premises. But in order for them to travel all the way to their work in Johannesburg as well as get all the work done in time, they had to leave Soweto in the early morning darkness.

Something that always disturbed me about this early departure was the fact that my mother, when her cousin was not around, had to walk alone to the bus stop in the darkness. At that time, Diepkloof was still known as "Dark City". The idea that she was out there alone disturbed me, no matter how young I was. I knew she had to go through passages and deserted spots where anything could happen. So, on those occasions when she had to walk alone, I always felt afraid for her.

Anyway, on the day of Ausie Margaret, Mma Moretlwa's daughter's wedding, Levi and I were there. It was a great wedding and they even had a band playing. But it did not outclass the wedding we saw a year before next door to my mother's distant niece, Ausie Binki, who was the wife of Ntate Molatlhegi, the man who had driven my father everywhere when he was ill. What was unforgettable about that wedding was the cars. They had hired three Jaguar XJ6's for the occasion. It was the first time I had seen a Jaguar in the streets of Zone Four, and three of them on top of that, each zigzagging slowly and proudly from one side of the road to the other.

Anyway, back to the wedding of Ausie Margaret, Mma Moretlwa's daughter. My mother was one of the women in the social club in charge of the cooking on the open coal fire. When I became aware of that, I approached her for food. She swiftly organised a plate for Levi and myself. It was ting-ya-mabele – sorghum pap – and mogodu – tripe – and she really heaped on the mogodu. I was used to eating meat as tiny as my two little fingers. So that day Levi and I feasted on the ting and mogodu. I was glad that she was there and could easily get food like that, unlike at other weddings where we knew no one and had to wait our turn and accept what was dished up.

That evening, as soon as I arrived home, my mother started to shout at me.

"How could you do that to me?" she said. "How could you come and pester me for food like ntja ya moghodoi – a hungry mongrel – which has not been fed in weeks? Do you have any idea how embarrassing it was? Before all my friends, you coming there, dirty as you were, asking for food like ngwana o robalang malunde – a street kid – who never gets food at home?"

As she spoke, I felt the pain in her voice. My mother was definitely hurt by my actions. At the wedding it appeared so normal, but as she explained it now, I was getting a completely different picture of what I did. Especially after the countless warnings she had given me about eating out and especially at people we did not know. "I hate a child who eats all over the show as if I do not feed him," she used to say. "Even if he is poisoned, we will never know where exactly he was poisoned." So, following my gluttony at Mma Moretlwa's daughter's wedding, it became clear to me that I had dishonoured my mother. "Have you ever seen any one of my children eating all over the place, or asking for food at weddings, have you?" she continued hammering at me. "Or have you now adopted your friend's bad ways of eating everywhere?" My mother was referring of course to Levi.

Levi ate at our house almost every day. On weekends, he would be on the doorstep the moment I woke up. He knew more or less the time we drank tea, as well as the time we ate lunch and supper, especially during the summer. It had never occurred to me that my mother might not approve of me sharing my food with Levi. After all, it was she who instilled in us, her children, the notions of goodwill and sharing. Whatever my mother brought home from work, she made sure it was shared equally among all the children. She would bring home two apples and they would be divided into eight quarters, a quarter for everyone. And then there was the point of cleanliness, which she also instilled into us. "You can't just go and give it to your brothers with your dirty hands," she would warn my sisters, if they were passing us a snack. "Put it on a bread plate, don't you know these people ke basebetsi." – They are workers.

The only time foods were not equally shared was when my mother brought home a single little sweet. And in that case it came straight to me, the last-born. You see, my people had a saying of which I enjoyed the benefits. The saying was "Moja-morago ke kgosi" – The one who eats last is king. And since I was the last one to come into this world in my family, I was the "king" and I always won the little favours from my mother.

But my mother was very strict when it came to me showing respect for my brothers and sisters, even if I was "mamma's baby". I was often punished for confusing being last-born with being always right. I thought that because I was the last-born and the favourite in the house, I could just talk and do as I liked, especially with my two sisters. "You must count your words when you talk to your sisters," was a statement my mother often uttered while she was either pinching my ear or when I was running away from the peach tree stick. And of course my two sisters were experts when it came to organising the stick for my lashings.

But back to sharing food. When my mother apportioned a chicken in the house, she always took age and position into consideration. My two oldest brothers, Motsietsi and Moropa, were given a thigh each. My next oldest brother, Kgofa, and my sister, Lesego, were handed drumsticks. Gilbert got the front part, the breast, because it was easy to handle. My mother served herself up the back of the chicken, while my sister Pontsho and I each received a wing. If the chicken was slaughtered at home, I received special favours and was also given the head and neck. I must say, it was one hell of an exercise to find meat on either the head or the neck of a chicken. But I learnt early how to negotiate my way through the crevices of these bony parts of the chicken like an expert.

Generally, what I enjoyed most about chicken was to chew the juicy marrow out of the bones. But chewing the bones alone was never as rewarding as eating pap and chewing the bones at the same time. If you have ever had the opportunity to experience eating such a mixture you will forever revere the prowess of the human mouth and brain. The oral acrobatics and contortions that went on during such an activity were phenomenal. What we used to do was to chew bones on one side of the mouth and pap on the other side. We then somehow, with our tongues, extracted the juice from the crushed bones, filtered it, and then transported the juice with the tongue to the other side of the mouth to be mixed in with the pap. We then had to make sure to block the bony fragments from sliding down the throat as we carefully swallowed the tasty mixture of pap and bone juice. It was during this phase of the operation that absolute care had to be taken, as you might end up swallowing bone fragments, which could hurt or even choke you. Having successfully swallowed the nourishing pap-juice mixture, you could then spit out the bone fragments. I bet there is no school in the world which could teach children how to execute such a delicate operation inside one's mouth ... but we did just that.

But to get back to the point of my mother's tongue-lashing the day of Mma Moretlwa's daughter's wedding: it was because of her words and the pain I had seen in her face that day, that I felt obliged to refuse Jimmy's mother's scrumptious cake. Yes, I was well rewarded in praise from Jimmy's mother for saying no, but to this day my tongue still hankers after that piece of cake I had to sit and watch my friends greedily licking their fingers over.

1976: The "Power" and visiting Pylkop

When my sister returned home from school one cold day in mid-June, she told us that things were bad in deep-Soweto. Although Diepkloof was part of Soweto, we referred to the rest of Soweto as deep-Soweto. Diepkloof was like an outpost due east of Soweto. Lesego at the time was at school in Orlando, which was adjacent to Diepkloof.

"Students are fighting with soldiers in the streets out there," she announced excitedly to Pontsho and me as she was busy ironing her dungarees for school the next day.

"Do soldiers have guns?" I asked.

"They were shooting at the students," she dismissed me with a serious voice. "And the students were stoning them. The boys were the ones leading the way and they had rubbish bin lids and bricks as they fought the soldiers."

I looked at my sister and thought, Does she really think that I am that stupid? I mean, I had been going to the movies for the past three years now. I had seen movies like Kelly's Heroes, The Dirty Dozen, Five For Hell, From Hell to Victory, To Hell and Back, and I had seen what soldiers' guns could do. I had seen them ripping through people from a great distance. And now she was expecting me to believe stone-throwing boys standing up to soldiers' bullets. I would have to see that before I could believe it, I thought.

1976: THE "POWER" AND VISITING PYLKOP

The next day – which was June 17, 1976 – all the students at school were talking about what was happening in deep-Soweto. In fact, it was all anyone was talking about.

"They say some students have been killed," Dan Masiba, a classmate, said.

"They also say that some white soldiers have been killed," another boy who was in our group added, as we waited for the morning school bell to ring for first assembly.

Suddenly my sister Lesego's reports from the previous day began to strike true. But the idea of students being killed shocked me. It sent my head into a spin and all of a sudden I felt unsafe. The only students I could recall ever dying were in accidents or had suffered sickness – they had not been gunned down by soldiers. The thought that I could be walking along my street and suddenly a soldier could creep up and shoot me was frightening, like a movie gone wrong.

That day we were let out of school early – another signal that the stories we were hearing were true. But on the whole, for me, getting out of school early merely presented a golden opportunity to go home and finish the wire car I was busy constructing. As soon as I arrived home – safely, without any soldiers firing at me – I went to work on my car with Gilbert, my brother, as my coach. Gilbert by then was no longer at school, due, in no small part, to the impatience and complete lack of support from most of his teachers. I was hardly even aware that he had speech problems, perhaps because I had grown up in the same house as him and thought his speech impediment was simply his particular way of speaking. It was only after I started school and people began asking me how I managed to understand what he was saying, that I realised not only did Gilbert have a physical disability, he also did not speak normally. Gilbert's disability was the result of a childhood accident, and my mother used to say to me, "Your brother came back very far when he was injured." I could not understand what she really meant; I guess the fact that I grew up seeing Gilbert walking differently, with his right arm and leg only partly functioning and his speech somewhat slurred, made me think it was almost normal. Unfortunately, unlike his lower primary school teachers, Gilbert's higher primary school teachers were impatient with him and some of them even mocked and made fun of him. As a result, my folks decided to take him out of school. He was better off at home.

Gilbert said to me now, "In order to make a nice-looking car you have to make sure that all your wires are straightened out before you start." Of course it took me ages to understand his approach. On previous occasions I had attempted to make wire cars using wire still crooked and bent, and had mostly failed. Now I was beginning to see Gilbert's point. I was busy with a Mercedes Benz "China-eyes", as we referred to this particular model.

Perhaps my most successful wire car to date was a Volkswagen Passat station wagon, but it disappeared shortly after I had finished it. At first I suspected Levi, even though he was my best friend. He was suspect number one because he was the only person who knew where I hid my car at night. Not only that, Levi could be unpredictable at times. I recall the day he stole a hen Gilbert was busy constructing for a school handiwork assignment. The incident took place on a Saturday morning, shortly after we had finished our tea. Gilbert had placed the hen, which was covered in mashed paper, just outside the kitchen door to dry out in the sun. Levi, out of the blue, swooped on my brother's handiwork and off he went. I gave chase down the street as he ran towards his house. I must say, for someone who was shorter and younger than me and carrying a rather heavy piece of artwork, he ran well. He outran me until he finally reached his kitchen door and I managed to catch up with him just as he tried to open it. Fortunately for me, his front door opened in two stages, which was especially hard to negotiate for someone as small as Levi. First you had to turn the knob and then you had to bump the door with your buttocks before you could actually get it open. It was during this manoeuvre that I cornered him. I recovered my brother's handiwork and did not speak to Levi for the rest of that day.

The following day he was back at our house as if nothing had happened and we were friends again. It did not even seem to bother him when my sister, Lesego, asked, "How dare you show your dirty face here after what you did yesterday?"

I was the one who came to the fore to protect him. "You leave my friend alone," I defended. "He did not steal your craftwork, so get off his case."

Now I was sitting next to Gilbert as he coached me through this voluntary assignment of mine to make a wire Mercedes Benz. Actually, this car was a sort of competition between myself and a boy called Seun. He and his group of friends were not very impressed with me when they noted that my previous car, the Volkswagen Passat, was better than the car they had just made, and now they were out to show me they could do better. So this time I was more than willing to heed Gilbert's advice.

"You must take extra care over the way you bend your wire for the front lights," he said, "because it is the front lights which will distinguish this model from the other Mercedes Benz cars."

Just as he gave that piece of advice, we heard a loud, whirring noise, like some large machine was hovering just above our roof. We immediately ran outside to have a look and saw it was an army helicopter. As kids, we had grown up with the idea that if a plane flew past we could shout at it for presents and sweets, as if the people inside could hear us and might eventually oblige. But this was the first time we had ever had a helicopter in our street, noisily just hovering above us. It was incredible, and scary.

The next thing I saw was people of all ages running for their yards. While I was trying to figure out what was happening, I felt something strong nip in my eyes, nose and throat. There was a thin pale of white smoke a few metres away from my house. "It's teargas," one older boy shouted as he ran past us. That was my first taste of teargas. The next thing I heard, in the distance, was the staccato of machine gun fire. At first I felt proud that I could recognise the sound from the movies, and then I thought about what my sister had said the day before and what everybody had said earlier at school today about students fighting with soldiers. Suddenly the sound of the guns made me uneasy and I retreated back behind my fence.

A little later, when the helicopter had disappeared from sight, I saw people carrying cases of beer, some on their shoulders, some on their bicycles and still others running along with cases of beer heaped onto wheelbarrows. Levi was among them.

"We must go back and get some more," Levi called out to me after he had dropped the box he was carrying off at his home. And when I did not respond he came right up to me. "Let's go and get some more," he urged, pulling me by my hand.

By this time there was a sense of high excitement and urgency as people were running up and down the street with different items. Many were carrying food in abundance in their arms and in wheelbarrows.

I put my "China-eyes" away carefully before I allowed Levi to drag me along.

"Where does all the stuff come from?" I asked. On the streets I saw small boys emptying the contents of brown bottles down their throats. I felt sick in the stomach as I remembered the sour taste of beer from some experiments I had tried in the past. Whenever there were visitors at our home who drank beer, after they were done, I would be asked to remove the empty bottles and put them outside in the coal storage box. But on a few occasions, what I did was to empty the last bit of beer from some of the bottles down my throat. Frankly, there was nothing enjoyable about the taste, and the last time I did it, I nearly vomited.

"The big brothers are burning the bar at Zone Three. They are also burning big grocery trucks. All these things, we're getting them mahala – free. And you know that truck which delivers bread and rolls and red cakes and sponge cakes and cream doughnuts and ..."

"Yes, yes!" I stopped Levi, feeling I needed no further encouragement and that I also had to get my hands on the freebies. Especially the cakes and the cool drinks.

The last time I had eaten a cream doughnut was a year before with Jimmy, who else? On that particular day I had gone with him to the shops and he bought a cream doughnut and a carton of fresh milk. As we returned from the shops it started raining and we made for Sedibeng sa Thuto school. We broke into one of the classrooms and sat there as Jimmy shared his goodies with me. As we were about to bite into the doughnut, the caretaker came by on his rounds. We had to duck under a desk and eat crouching as we were afraid he might come back. I must say, cream doughnut or no cream doughnut, I did not enjoy eating under those conditions. And now, running along with Levi, I saw the chance of finally satisfying myself on a cream doughnut.

But I was in two minds about going all the way. I had to decide, and quickly, whether to follow Levi and the other boys or pull back and go home. I remembered the time I was beaten at the mine dumps after my mother had warned me several times about playing there.

My mother had also frequently warned me with another saying: Phuduhudu e molala moleele, e tlhajwa ke marumo as sa e lebana – A steenbok with a long neck is maimed by spears not meant for it. I had seen it happening on one occasion at the Zone Four shops. There was a gang scuffle that day and bottles and bricks were flying all over the place. I was coming out of the dairy shop with a pint of milk and a loaf of brown bread under my arm. In front of me, I saw this boy pushing people aside in order to get a good look at what was happening. The next thing I saw was him screaming and bleeding like someone had opened a tap of blood on his forehead. As for me, I dashed home without looking back.

Now here I was, facing the dilemma of either going against my mother's warnings, which always turned out to be right, or following my boyish gut-feelings, which in most cases left me in trouble. In the end I decided to follow Levi and the other boys because failure to do so would brand me as either a "mamma's boy" or a coward.

I was very nervous as we neared the scene of the looting and conflict. The occasional sound of gunfire grew louder. At the same time the sound of chanting could be heard in the background. The smell of things burning hung in the air. The movement of people running up and down the streets, with and without goods, was chaotic, like a movie of crowds in fast motion.

"Black Power!" I started seeing boys and girls of all ages in school uniform with their fists in the air as they cried out loud, "Black Power!" In the distance, through the dust, I saw strange-looking green steel cars speeding all over the place and I started falling back from the group I was with. This does not look good, I thought to myself. I'll be damned if I'm going to move deeper into this confusion. Finally I made my decision: I was going back. I started to drop back from the crowd and returned home without telling Levi or the others.

The next morning I was awoken by the thundering voice of the huge Ausie Binki, my mother's niece, who was Ntate Molatlhegi's wife.

"Mmane" – she called my mother Mmane, which meant aunt – "my boys had their fists up." By this time Ausi Binki had both her massive arms raised above her head. "And they were crying Man-Power! Man-Power!" Now I was confused. What I heard yesterday was Black Power ... or was it Man-Power?

"I am telling you, Mmane, you should have seen how they gave those white soldiers a tough time." Her tone was that of a person who was heaping praise on the actions of the children. It was completely contrary to what we had been taught, that children who acted disrespectfully should be punished. I was astounded, but as events unfolded and were spoken about at home that day and in the days after, the penny began to drop. What was happening in our streets with the students was not ordinary disrespect; it had to do with people's rights and had the support of some parents.

The next day we went to school as usual. Before the morning bell rang, we were exchanging stories of what we saw, what happened, and what other people told us they saw or did.

"I was inside the beer hall yesterday," said Lot Dipane, a school friend of mine. Lot was a bit of a show-off who claimed that his karateka uncle once fought a tiger at the Johannesburg Zoo. At the time I actually believed him. Especially after he showed me photos of his uncle in his white gi and black belt. "My uncle once flew over my father's car while it was in motion," Lot also once claimed. He could never stop talking about his uncle's bravado, not for a moment. And the worst part was I believed it. How I wished I had an uncle I could boast about. The only person I used to boast about was my aunt ... not the one who worked in Killarney, but her husband. Oh yes, her husband was also my aunt. You see, in Setswana culture, my aunt's husband is also called my aunt and my uncle's wife is called my uncle. It was only later that I saw my forefathers had confronted the gender equity thing long before it became mainstream. Anyway, I liked the fact that he was a policeman, and given the fear that a police uniform generated in the township, I felt proud that he was my aunt.

Talking of uniforms, even security guards qualified as policemen in my boyhood eyes, just as long as they wore uniforms. There was this old man who lived down the street, five houses away from ours. We called him Malome, meaning uncle. He wore a security uniform, which we mistook for a police uniform, and he used to chase us around and we used to run away the way hooligans would run when they were being pursued by the police. Malome was not the only one in a uniform who played with us. There was also Ntate Mokoena, who spoke in a funny way, but always liked playing with small children. And then there was another old man, who wore a black uniform, who we simply called "Are-You-Ready", because that was the game he liked playing with us. The game went something like this:

"Are you ready?" he would ask.

"Yes, Sir!" we would reply.

"Are you ready?" he would ask again.

"Yes, Sir!" we would reply again.

"One-two-three-four!" he would count and on four we would all freeze. To us it was an exciting game and we enjoyed playing it.

Ta-Ya-Mo-Loma-Notshi was yet another old uniformed man we loved to play with. Every time he passed us on the streets, riding his bicycle and carrying a crate of "shake-shake" – the local name given to sorghum beer, which arose because you had to shake the carton a few times before you could drink it – we called out in rhythm with him:

Ta ya mo loma notshi
Ya mma di binne side
Jwale ke di-marble case!

Don't ask me what it meant, because I have no idea, all I knew was that we used to recite this short piece together with him when he passed by on his bicycle, and it was fun.

"Ijo, ijo, ijo ... you should have seen it!" Lot, my bragging friend, continued his tale of the beer hall that morning. "At one stage the lights went out in the beer hall and it was so dark we were walking into each other. Then, like a dim light peering out of the darkness, we saw a red face, and everyone automatically attacked it." Lot was demonstrating with his hands as I listened intently with my imagination working at full throttle.

"And then what?"

"The next thing we heard was the red face shouting back at us in a familiar voice. It was then we realised it was only Papi. Papi wa leswafe" – Papi the albino.

I laughed, at the same time thinking: "What would have happened if Papi was killed?" It was common belief at the time that albinos did not die, they simply disappeared – never to be seen again. To me, right then, I thought how interesting it would have been to see Papi disappearing right in front of everyone's eyes. Later, I formed a different view about albinos, well, after I saw the movie Whispering Death, with Christopher Lee pursuing an albino terrorist. In that movie I saw the albino dying rather than disappearing, and from then on I believed albinos died in the same way as everyone else.

"How can you trust everything you see in the movies?" one of my friends retaliated when I argued that albinos died like everyone else. "You know that what you see in the movies is all lies. I mean today a person is shot dead and the next week he appears in another movie, alive and well."

"Have you ever heard someone saying that an albino is getting buried somewhere?" someone else finally put a lid on the argument. And, of course, that argument left a lingering doubt in my mind for many years to come.

Later that day, once the excitement had died down and we were all in class, a new source of anxiety materialised. Our classroom was next to the main gate and we saw them first – two "hippos" with red faces inside. It was the first time we had ever seen the green, squashed-up-looking half-tanks that the South African Army used to quell riots from so close by. The men inside the hippos, dressed in camouflage uniforms, were sitting with their bodies half out of the vehicles and would have looked like they were on some sort of safari were it not for the machine guns tucked under their arms. War movies jumped into my mind, and I pictured bodies being blown apart and strewn all over the ground. Coupled with stories we had heard the previous day of toddlers being shot through the head by stray bullets while playing innocently in their homes, those hippos approaching was like staring a terrible death in the eyes.

As the hippos entered the school yard, my stomach did a backwards somersault, I am sure along with everyone else's, because at that moment anarchy broke loose. Our teacher tried to calm us down, explaining to us that the hippos and the armed men were not going to do anything to us. But all that we could think of was that these soldiers were shooting black students to death. In our panic, we pushed the teacher aside and ran out of the classroom screaming, "*Ijoo! Mma wee! Ke bao!*" while the distraught teacher called after us: "Stand still! Calm down! The soldiers are not going to touch you!"

As I ran past the teacher at the classroom door, all I could still picture in my head was the rat-a-tat-tat of machine gun fire and heaps of children's bodies lying all over the school yard, just like in the movies. Some students were so panicked they climbed through the windows. A girl jumping through a window was gouged by broken glass and I saw a piece of flesh hanging from her thigh. My stomach twisted in fright. Nobody stopped for her. We were all scattering in different directions as we were innocently initiated into the events of June 1976 that began in Soweto and would end in the deaths of hundreds of school kids across the country.

For us, in Diepkloof, the day we ran out of school was not the last of it. There were incidents every day, but I remember one incident a few weeks later in particular. While we were playing on the streets, a Datsun Laurel army vehicle appeared. Everyone knew that the soldiers who drove around in Datsun Laurels did not ask questions; they spoke the language of the gun. Luckily I was near home and I ran to get into my mother's house, followed by the boys I was playing with. Such was the reputation of the Datsun Laurels that alongside us, as we ran, we saw a couple of strange kids we had never met before. All of us made straight for my mother's bedroom and hid under the bed. We were all shaking, and as we lay there dead quiet, we suddenly heard the heavy footsteps of soldiers, as if they were walking around somewhere in the yard.

Then the sound of the footsteps moved off and after a while we all crept out from under the bed. We ran up to the window and peeped through it. Almost out of nowhere, we saw two burly white soldiers running with one of the young boys who had been out on the street. He was a couple of years older than me, I'd say about fourteen. The soldiers held the boy by each of his arms and were running as fast as they could towards a clump of trees. When they got to the trees they did not stop but rammed him against the trunk of a tree whose diameter was twice the width of the boy. I had never witnessed such cruelty in my life. I had to shake my head several times to make sure I was neither dreaming nor watching a movie. The soldiers walked off casually and then drove off, leaving the boy bleeding under the big tree. Some people from the neighbouring houses ran out to help the boy. Up to this day, every time I see that boy, now a grown man with a scarred face, the scene repeats itself in my head just like it happened yesterday.

Towards the end of that year another scourge struck Soweto. Students of all ages were disappearing from the township. Most of them, we knew, were being taken into police custody. It was this threat, of being summarily removed from home and chucked into some unknown jail, as well as the ongoing unrest and school boycotts, that prompted my mother to send me, Gilbert and my two sisters to her younger brother's home in the country, to a place called Phadi, near Ramokokastad, in Bophutatswana – now North West Province.

I enjoyed the lifestyle in the country, or the "rural areas", as the farm areas were known, but I have to admit I did not always appreciate having to go out into the wilderness to fetch wood or look for donkeys or cattle. What I loved most was going with my uncle on a tractor to plough the fields. Firstly, we did not have to walk and,

Sedibeng sa Thuto Lower Primary School, which was opposite our home. The big tree in the middle is the very one used by the soldiers in 1976.

secondly, we could sit on the tractor all day as he drove up and down. I also liked the lunch which the field owners prepared for him. Some of them would prepare a whole chicken with pap and gravy. And sometimes there would even be beef or lamb.

My clearest memory of the country, though, involved a boy named Pyl. He was "The Man", or rather the menace, of the village – until "the Sowetans" arrived. "The Sowetans" were myself, Gilbert, Pontsho and Lesego, as well as my two cousins, Seuntjie and Agnes, who were sent to the country along with us. Seuntjie was four years older than me while Agnes and I were the same age.

Pyl was terrorising the entire village, generally making a nuisance of himself by bullying those weaker than himself and threatening to beat up old and young alike. To make matters worse, there was not much concerned parents could do, because of the protection Pyl received from his own parents. But he crossed the wrong line when he thought he could stand toe to toe with Seuntjie. What he did not know was that Seuntjie was associated with the notorious Jaws gang and knew a thing or two about street fighting.

We all gathered at the scene when Seuntjie said enough was enough and challenged Pyl to a fight. Pyl thought he had yet another easy victim before him. In the event, we all watched in horror but awe as Seuntjie drew a knife and with a few quick-flowing movements lightly slashed a now shivering and frightened "village terror". Pyl's cries were so loud the whole village thought he was being murdered.

Soon the police were investigating the case, and a few officers came around to my uncle's place. They started questioning my sister, Lesego, who tried hard to keep her cool.

"But you are not from here," one of the policemen commented. "I can hear from the way you speak that you must be from Gauteng." Johannesburg was then known as Gauteng.

As my sister tried to adjust her accent and language to sound like that of the local folk, I thought to myself, jail, here we come. I felt like running away when I thought of the stories of students who were taken into custody never to be seen again. In the end the police left Lesego alone, but only after my "uncle" – my uncle's wife – intervened.

Seuntjie, however, was arrested soon after, and ended up going through the justice system. He was sentenced to several lashes. But the day that Seuntjie the Sowetan had stood up to Pyl was the day that Pyl's reign of terror ended.

Early the following year, at the start of the new school year, we returned from "Pylkop", as we had begun to call the place. I was disappointed when I arrived home to find Levi had also been sent to the rural areas. I missed him so much, I just wanted to see him. But it was not to be until a year later.

Meeting my friends at school after about five months away was like a dream. There were some, like Levi, who did not return until later, and there were others who did not return at all. Most of us who had been sent away to the country had stories to tell about where we had been. I, for one, was proud to explain to my school friends how to milk a cow as well as a goat, the easiest way of catching a chicken and ringing its neck, and how to drive a donkey cart.

But there was one embarrassing moment while we were at Phadi that I was not going to share with my friends. It concerned the day a certain girl called Tumi, who lived nearby, came looking for me. I had never even spoken to her before, but she turned up and claimed that she was my girlfriend. In a little village news travels fast. And I, a late bloomer and private person, ignorant in the ways of love, was furious. Everyone, from my uncle and aunt down to my cousins, brother and sisters, had a good laugh. In my eyes, Tumi had turned me into a laughing stock. I was enraged, so infuriated and humiliated I cried.

Actually, that was not the only story I was not prepared to share. There was another sad story which I did not want my friends to know about. It was the story of Letlamoreng. Letlamoreng was the village brick-maker. He was a jolly friendly elderly man who always greeted me with a smile when he saw me. I remember his brown overalls and brown boots which were always stained with cement. He had a face that shone and looked like he could not hurt a fly. They said he lived all alone. One morning we woke up to the news that he had hung himself. I was shattered. I could not understand what would make such a friendly elderly man do such a thing. The more I thought about why he had done it, the more I saw his smiling face before me.

A few days later I learnt that he had raped a little girl.

But still, at that age, I did not understand the concept of rape very well, and found it difficult to accept this as an explanation for suicide. I recalled hearing of people back home who committed suicide, but none of the stories ever involved rape.

Once, I even witnessed someone trying to commit suicide. He was stopped just in time. His name was Scooter and he lived down the street from our house. One day, I saw people running towards the mine dumps. When I asked what was going on, the answer was, "Scooter is going to the trees and he has an axe." In my little head I did not see anything wrong with that. People often went to the area near the mine dumps to chop down eucalyptus trees for firewood and medicinal purposes. It was not until I heard, "Scooter is going to chop himself to death," that I, too, decided to follow the crowd.

I was more interested in the technique Scooter was going to use to chop his own head off than in the fact that Scooter was planning to take his own life. I had seen chickens being beheaded, and I had seen people being beheaded in the movies, but I had never heard of a man beheading himself. At that age, I really believed it was possible.

Of course, Scooter was stopped by the bystanders and today he is still alive. But since that day, whenever I saw him, I wondered how he was going to chop his own head off with an axe.

The bell rang. It was the first school day of 1977. At morning assembly, we were told that we were going to write exams before any teaching started. We had heard rumours that we were going to have to write exams, to test whether we should go on to the next grade, because of the number of kids who had missed school since the events of June 1976, but it wasn't till that first morning that we knew for sure. The exams were written over a period of about a week, and a couple of weeks later when the results were made available, we had all passed. That meant we could proceed to Standard Five. To me it was like a miracle. To return to school after being away for almost five months, only to write examinations I had not even studied for, and to pass, well, that was great. How I wish we could have "Power" every year, I thought silently. "Power" was the thing for me if it meant being allowed to stay away from school for so long only to come back and pass into the next grade. The "Day of Power", as most kids referred to June 16, was definitely the day for me.

But that year much the same pattern developed as the previous year. Many kids, including myself and most of those in my Standard Five class, started to disappear from school from around mid-year, only to return at the beginning of the following year, 1978. This "disappearance" came as a result of ongoing clashes between the township's hostel dwellers, who were assisted by the security forces, and the township residents. The fighting and bloodshed brought destabilisation to the township and made the streets in many areas unsafe. In 1977 students also took to burning their Bantu Education school books and many a school was destroyed. Education in the township was in chaos and many of us began to see going to school as a waste of time, especially going to schools that had been gutted by fire. In winter, going to a school with no windows, it was too cold to concentrate. It seemed easier to keep ourselves warm in the streets than in class. It was also much more fun. Actually, being away from school gave boys like me the opportunity to play until we dropped. Not surprisingly, I suppose, my mother was not happy with my not going to school. She insisted that I at least go to school on a daily basis to check what was going on.

"Mma, I cannot go near the school premises," I used to explain in a rebellious tone, "I cannot take the chance of being killed by the soldiers or Mazola a ko hostel – Zulus living in hostels. I'm still small. Apart from that, it is still 'Power'."

"But you are not small when you gallivant across the township the whole day, looking for I-don't-know-what," my mother yelled back at me. "Tomorrow when I return from work I want you to tell me what was going on at school. I have a good mind to go and see your class teacher about this." Fortunately for me, as with many other children, my mother did not find the time to visit the school, as missing a day's work was a loss of badly needed wages.

I was beginning to enjoy loafing so much that it was becoming a way of life for me, so much so that I and many kids like me were losing any interest in going to school at all.

Sometimes my friends and I would gather around and sing the freedom songs we had heard being sung all over the township. There was one song that made my flesh feel all goosebumpy. The song, sung in Zulu, stirred emotions inside of me I could not understand. The part that especially raised strong feelings in me went like this:

The Black thing
That pulls by the chain
What went wrong?
The dogs will be slaughtered!

There is the hippo
Gunning down the Azanians
What have we done?
The dogs will be executed!

There are the soldiers
Shooting down at the Africans
What have we done?
The dogs will be slain!

I pictured blacks being pulled along by chains that were hung around their necks, just like in the movies about slavery that I had seen. In my head I saw innocent children slain by the guns of callous soldiers, and something inside of me felt sick and dispirited. Young as I was, I knew that what was happening at that time was not right, even if I could not explain why I thought that. People died on our streets on a weekly basis before 1976, but I felt inside of me that the deaths coming in the wake of June 1976 were different from the ones before. The haunting line in the song was, What have we done?

The beginning of 1978, when we had to go back to school again, turned out to be different from the year before when we simply wrote a few exams and we all passed into the next grade. This time all the Standard Fives in our school failed except for one girl. At that time Standard Five was a certificate level grade and therefore the exam was "external", that is, set by the department for all children in Standard Five. We did not even know that, and those of us who did, did not care. Our excuse, as for anything to do with school, was, "It's Black Power and we cannot go to school. You want the police and soldiers to shoot at us or the students to burn us in class?"

As a result, because of the huge number of Standard Five failures, in 1978 we had double the number of Standard Five classes. Now we and the Standard Fours, who had managed to pass in the same way as we did the year before, were all lumped together in the same classrooms. This was to be the toughest year of my school life. We had to attend school in gutted classrooms, with no windows, squeezed around a few desks. In winter it was so cold we had to make mbawula – fire made in an open drum – in the classroom to keep warm. In order to keep the fire burning, the boys were constantly sent out to fetch coal and look for firewood during school hours.

And there was another thing: the teachers were more hostile than ever before, as if taking revenge for what was done to some of them in the aftermath of 1976. Some of the teachers were beaten up by students during the unrest for trying to maintain the status quo. Corporal punishment now exceeded anything we had known before. As protection against the teacher's cane, I ended up wearing two shirts, including a T-shirt, three jerseys, and two pairs of trousers to school. As you may gather from the number of shirts and jerseys I wore, the in thing for punishment at that time was caning across the back. But there were still a good few teachers who preferred the buttocks, even for girls. I felt sorry for the girls because we had the advantage of doubling if not trebling the number of trousers we wore. They, of course, merely wore tunics. But the teachers were not that stupid, they were aware of us boys doubling our trousers, so they increased the intensity of their blows when it came to caning the boys.

Some boys came up with some interesting ideas to combat these canings. I remember this little short boy in our class, who was so terrified of the cane that one day he decided to put a thick exercise book in his pants. The teacher split the book in two with his cane. To the boy's dismay it was a biology notebook and we were well into the third quarter of the year. Can you imagine all the drawings of cells, insects like locusts, animals and other life-forms, apart from all the written notes, he had to redo?

At the end of the year, most of those who were repeating Standard Five passed, me included.

Goodbye to boyhood

In 1979 I started high school. My dream had always been to go to Madibane High School. Just like at Ikaneng Lower Primary and Tlotlego Higher Primary, my surname was well known at Madibane. Moropa, Kgofa and Lesego had all gone to school there, and I knew the benefits that came from teachers who knew your older brothers and sisters, especially if they had done well, as mine had done. Unfortunately it was not to be. That year, students from Tlotlego Higher Primary School were sent on to Namedi Junior Secondary School, which was opposite Madibane High School.

The first thing that unsettled me about high school was the mixture. For eight years I had gone to school with pupils from one language group, and that was Setswana. Now all of a sudden I found myself in the same class with pupils from six different language groups: Zulu, Tswana, Sotho, Pedi, Xhosa, and Tsonga. At first, we formed allegiances based on our old school ties and the language bond. But as time passed, we began to identify and form friendships with kids who lived near to us, irrespective of former school or language group. Before we knew it, we were speaking a concoction of languages which catered to almost all the languages in the class.

On the whole, high school came as a surprise to me. I was not fully prepared to enter into puberty. I was in shock when I discovered that I had to give up the wire horse and trailer I had finished towards the end of the previous year. I was equally uneasy to learn that I had to abandon most of the friends I had known for a very long time.

I remember Patty, a high school mate, standing next to me after school one day as I was busy playing with my old school friends. We were playing with our wire cars just outside my house. Patty called me away from my friends, and said: "O etsa'ng monna?" – What in heaven's name are you doing?

I looked at my friends, then back at Patty, trying to figure out what I could be doing wrong.

"Wa hlanya, monna!" – Are you out of your mind! he said with a rigid, disturbed-sounding voice, as though trying to shout at the same time as keeping his voice down.

I looked up at Patty. He was bigger and taller than me. It was his second year at high school and he was, therefore, my senior. He lived a street away from me, and because of school we had become friendly.

"What?" I asked.

He indicated with his head towards my friends who were now throwing sand at each other. I was feeling impatient with Patty as I wanted to go and join in the fun.

"You can't play like that anymore," he said. "You are at high school now. O grootman ya tsona ntwana tseo – A big brother to those boys. And you should stop behaving like a little boy and start acting like a man. Can you imagine what will happen if those beautiful young cherries – girls – at school see you playing like this?"

I slowly lowered my eyes and caught sight of my pale feet protruding from my short pants. I imagined myself standing before a number of beautiful young girls I had noticed at school over the past few weeks, and felt my heart beating fast.

I was not sure whether the speed of my heartbeat was a result of the shock that came from visualising my weedy physical appearance in relation to those well-formed girls at school, or whether it was due to the sudden realisation that I was standing at the edge of a precipice which I could feel myself about to cross, never to come back.

It was bad enough that I had to start wearing long grey trousers to school rather than the short pants, shirt, and no shoes that I was accustomed to. I just could not understand that I was also expected to leave everything I held dear, just like that. What about my friends who I had known most of my life? Did it mean I could never play games such as cowboys and Indians with them again, a game which we used to play across the length and breadth of the school grounds next to my house? What about my home-made Mercedes Benz "China eyes" and the horse and trailer I had just finished making? How could I walk away from them? Did it also mean goodbye to eghie, bhati, ma-rounders, di-beke, skop-di-bolo?

When I came back to my senses, Patty was gone. I looked at my friends who were still playing in the road and I joined them. In my heart I said to myself, Today I will play until I drop. Tomorrow, when I wake up, I will know what to do.

The issue of cherries took up my thoughts as I was playing. I thought about the black school shoes I had to wear to school every day, even when it was hot, and how those shoes had to shine, otherwise what would the girls say? All of a sudden the opinion of girls was the yardstick for the reputation of the boys. The smell of my armpits had never been an issue until then. Luckily, with the caddying work I had recently managed to get, I had increased my spending money from five cents a day to fifty cents a day, and sometimes even more. On a good weekend I could make up to eight rand from caddying. So I managed to buy a cheap roll-on deodorant, which I still had to remind myself to apply every day.

There were a few girls who looked at me and just smiled. It took time for me to accept that such things happened. At first I was worried that maybe they thought I was funny or I was some kind of joke. There was this girl in my class, Mmalesego, who was beautiful. Her beauty scared the living daylights out of me. She was one of those who kept smiling when she looked at me.

"Go talk to her," Patty once advised me. "I think she likes you."

Talk to her about what? I thought at the time. But maybe Patty was right, I thought to myself now.

Only a few days ago, Patty had told me that there were girls who were giving me the eye. Perhaps if I listened to Patty, he would throw in a word or two on my behalf? Who knows, maybe things would turn out better than they did with Nokuthula?

There was one girl who made me feel really good whenever I looked at her. She was one I felt I had to go and talk to. She was in Form One A and I was in Form One F, six classrooms away from hers. I did not know her name or what language she spoke. Yet I felt her presence each day through all those classroom walls that separated us. I didn't even have any idea where she lived. But whenever I saw her during breaks, it made me feel warm inside. I did not know, or understand, what brought on those feelings; all I knew was that it was always good to see her. I ended up making sure that during our short breaks between lessons I would walk past her classroom just to get a glimpse of her. I really wanted to speak to her, even though I had absolutely no idea what I would say. These, yes these, were some of the factors – thanks to Patty and the girl who stole my heart – that eventually made me gently surrender my boyhood and embrace puberty.

JANUARY, 2000
SOSHANGUVE

WORD LIST

abuti – brother
ausie – older sister, from Afrikaans *ousie*
bhati – game played with a tennis ball on a course drawn on the road. Two teams participate. The ball must be kicked through the competing team's defence line. If the ball gets through, rounds are run, and with a certain number of rounds, the game is won. If the ball is caught, the player who kicked it is sent off until all players are eliminated and sides are changed.
black maipatile – hide and seek
blom – to hang out, from Afrikaans *flower*
chachas – burning plastic
cherry – girl
chomi – variant of *chommie* – friend
clap – blow to the face, from Afrikaans *klap*
di-beke – game in which two players try to hit an opposing player in the middle of a circle with a tennis ball. If the player in the middle manages to avoid being hit and the ball goes past the throwers, rounds are run by his team, while the other team tries to hit them with the ball to take them out of the game. The game is won once a certain number of rounds are completed.
dumela – good day
eghie – game in which each player is assigned a number. Eghie one starts the game by calling a number and throwing the ball into the air. The one whose number is called tries to catch the ball. If he fails, he has to hit another player with the ball. This player now throws the ball and shouts a number. If the first player fails to hit another player, he is accorded a penalty. Once a single player has a certain number of penalties, he is chased and smeared with coal ash.
fahfi – variant of *fah-fee*, illegal Chinese gambling game
fia-fia or fia-go – fair fist fight
gamors – rubbish, from Afrikaans *gemors*
gazaat – club together
ghoni – type of knife
go-fetjane – last born
go-teka – game involving kicking a tennis ball
hei wena – hey you

keti – from cattie, short for catapult
kwela-kwela – police van
konfyt – jam
laetie – variant of *lighty* or *lightie*, meaning youngster or child. In this case, it refers to younger brother.
lebebe – thick layer that forms on top of milk that has been boiled
legwala – to be a coward, from the isiZulu *igwala*
ma vra wao wao – swearing on your mother's reproductive organs
ma-bare-bare – grape vine
majaja – unfashionable, ugly clothes
makgaritla – left-overs
malome – uncle
mangulungulu – township name for any big motorcar, from *khulu*, isiZulu for big
mbawula – fire made in an open drum
mmane – aunt
mmasepala – municipality
mogudo – tripe
motswala – cousin
seruwa – chamber pot
shuu! – exclamation
Six Mabone – six lights, township name for a car with six tail lights like a Dodge Monaco
skoti – hole in the ground where stolen products were hidden, from *umgodi*, isiZulu for hole
skroplap – rag for washing floors
sosaete – social club, from *society*
spara-para – running zig-zag down mine dumps
spyt – enema, from *spuit*, Afrikaans for syringe
strepi – striped rat, from *strepie*, Afrikaans for stripe
tlhogo – head
Valaza – township name for a Valiant motorcar
Wa phapha wena – you are too big for your boots
ye-belungu – "belonging to the white man" – in this case referring to a peanut butter sandwich with a glass of milk